Discovering Welsh Houses

A guide to eighteen architectural gems, based on the BBC television series.
Written and photographed by **Michael Davies**

GRAFFEG

in association with

Contents

Introduction

In the summer of 2005 I was made an offer I couldn't refuse – to travel around Wales looking at and talking about Welsh houses.

I have been working as a chartered architect for more than twenty years, the greater part of which has been spent specialising in historic buildings conservation, mostly throughout Wales. During this time I have been lucky enough to have come across some of Wales' most fascinating and historic houses. It is the sort of 'hands-on' education you can't glean from a book alone, and for me it is the best way of discovering the delights of our built heritage. In the summer of 2005 I was made an offer I couldn't refuse – to travel around Wales looking at and talking about Welsh houses. What an offer! Besides worrying about how I was going to fit it into an already busy work life, it took me no time at all to agree. Alfresco TV had come up with the idea for the BBC, and they needed an architectural expert to accompany their presenter in making the programme. I had never done any television before, except for the odd interview, and was excited, and nervous, by the prospect.

The programme has given me the opportunity to look at forty-five different houses around all parts of Wales

West Usk Lighthouse, page 36; Sunningdale Tŷ Draw Road, page 106; Treowen, page 116; Penwhilwr, page 18.

The programme has given me the opportunity to look at forty-five different houses around all parts of Wales, from a very simple stone cottage, to a 52 roomed Victorian mansion. Each programme showed three houses linked by a common theme – such as Coastal Living, Keeping it in the Family, Labour of Love, and so on. There were three main elements we looked for in each house – 1. social history, 2. architecture, 3. the current owners. Therefore, we didn't just film any house. It had to be strong in one or two of these three elements. Inevitably some themes, and some houses were stronger than others, but overall we managed to find a whole variety of different and interesting places to visit. However, two things stood out for me. The people themselves, and their stories of courage and tenacity in achieving their goals; and, the locations of some of the houses.

Cynefin, set in a stunning location with the Snowdonia mountains behind.

Many of the houses we visited were in stunning locations, and it didn't really matter how good the house was architecturally, because the location was so amazing. But when you had both location and architecture, then you knew you were looking at one of the best houses in the country.

One of the best examples of architecture and location we looked at was a new house called 'Cynefin' near Towyn in North Wales (page 70). The house is set in a rolling landscape with dramatic mountains in the distance, one of which is Cadair Idris. The building has been carefully designed so that it has a real sense of place, something you actually feel as you walk through the building; you make a real connection with the building, and it connects with you. It is amazing to think that, at a time when many people have lost confidence in the design of new buildings, this building was a big hit. It was probably most people's favourite house over the three series. Another favourite was 'Sarn Badrig' near Harlech, also known as the 'Chocolate House' because of its connections with the Cadbury family. This is a very modest house, but set on the coast overlooking miles of sandy beach leading up to the Llŷn Peninsula.

Whilst I was able to help unravel the architectural story of each house for the viewers, I was also able to learn so much more myself. Studying houses seems to have become a great British obsession, and here in Wales we are no different. We have a great passion for our cultural identity in Wales. I suppose we are all experts when it comes to houses. After all, if the best way to study a subject is to live and breath it for many years, then we have all spent a lifetime studying houses, maybe not academically but in a 'hands-on' sort of way. As a practicing architect I am often asked to design a new house for someone and, despite taking seven years to qualify, it's the one area where you can sometimes feel no more of an expert than your client. It often begins with your client unfolding a piece of lined paper in front of you, proudly displaying their attempts at designing their dream home – sometimes two Barrett homes stuck together. But as the design process unfolds it's very gratifying to have your client appreciate that good design is still an art, and only practiced by a few.

But if we truly want to understand what makes a good house we must look back to our history, and study the evolution of where we have come from...

But if we truly want to understand what makes a good house we must look back to our history, and study the evolution of where we have come from, how we have shaped our architectural landscape and how architecture has influenced our culture, a culture that is very different to the rest of Britain. This is reflected in our buildings – buildings and culture influencing each other.

The description of Welsh houses has often been simplified suggesting that we are a nation of white render and slate roofs, with very few houses of distinction. But if you look carefully throughout this small hilly country you will see a rich diversity of building styles and materials, albeit in a less flamboyant style compared to England. But there is good reason for this. Wales has always been a relatively poor nation, under severe pressures with a small and sparsely scattered population. Its landscape and climate have made it difficult to create wealth. The lack of easy transport and dealing with continuous conflict and occupation has resulted in smaller, less opulent houses.

Wales is a small nation with a huge variety of landscape, and this is reflected in its buildings. As transport through such a landscape was difficult, you tended to build from what you could find around you and dig out of the ground, or cut from the trees. This provided the vernacular for a variety of locations around Wales. The colour and texture of stone varies considerably from one area to another. The light grey Lias Limestone of the Vale of Glamorgan, the orange-brown Pennant Sandstone of the South Wales Valleys, and the Old Red Sandstones of Brecon. The stone in many areas of North Wales bears a striking resemblance to the slate that is so abundant to the area, but used as a building stone rather than roofing material.

The age and hardness of the rock often determined its use, and how easily it could be broken, chiselled or carved. This is reflected in the appearance of the building, with the bigger boulders being laid at the bottom courses of the building, becoming smaller in the higher courses where it was more difficult to lift into place. Larger cornerstones would also offer great stability to the structure. These practical measures also provided scale and dignity to a building, which can act upon the senses in a subliminal way. This concept can be seen in the great temples built by the Greeks, where visual balance and correcting optical illusions in the search for perfection became a great preoccupation. Similarly, when slating a roof in diminishing courses. Whilst this provided a very elegant roof covering, with the slates becoming smaller as they rose up the roof and further way from the eye, it was also practical to use up your larger slates on the lower parts of the roof and finish off with the smaller pieces and off-cuts at the top of the roof.

House building is completely different today. The majority of new houses pay little regard to the use of local materials and styles.

In some parts of Wales houses were predominantly built of timber frame as good building stone was not readily available nearby. Many of these have now vanished, but if you look carefully you can still see remnants of timber construction in the external walls, and buried even deeper within the structure of the building. Many of these timber buildings were built over, leaving the frame in place when adding stone or brick walls. One of the houses I visited was a stone cottage called 'Hafod Y Garreg' near Builth Wells (page 57). Buried in a first floor wall is a magnificent timber cruck frame truss, the only visible timberwork from the original building. When this timber was analysed using dendrochronology, it was found to belong the oldest surviving house in Wales.

House building is completely different today. The majority of new houses pay little regard to the use of local materials and styles.

Above left: Welsh slate roof laid in diminishing courses.
Above right: Thatched roof over lime render.
Below left: Oak frame with pegged joints.
Below right: Stone walling from north Wales.

Consequently, houses no longer have a sense of belonging or regional identity. There is much talk of constructing 'green' buildings, and yet many of the building materials we use are brought in from a great distance, using unnecessary energy for transport. Surely it makes sense to use local materials again if we really want to use sustainable building methods. There is so much we can learn from our past. Look at how a simple old cottage used small windows on its north side to protect itself from the cold winds, and larger windows on the south to capture the sunlight. This was 'green' building centuries ago.

I remember starting out as a sixteen year old working in an architects office, and meeting a retired architect who use to work for the practice. He must have been in his eighties and was quite frail. He passed on a piece of advice that has stayed with me all these years. He said that architecture is a huge and wonderful subject, and even though he was of a great age he was still learning, because you will never know it all. You must keep learning. It has taken many years but I now understand what he meant. I am continually learning about architecture, and feel I have only just scratched the surface. *Discovering Welsh Houses* has given me the opportunity to add to my knowledge, and to meet some wonderful and interesting people along the way.

1

Llaeniau
Tŷ Un Nos – 'One Night House'

Visiting this little house was quite a journey from our base in Cardiff. We travelled up to the north west part of Wales on the Llŷn Peninsula, high up on a hill with views over the mountains of Snowdonia and in the other direction, all the way out to Ireland over the sea.

North west Wales on the Llŷn Peninsula.

Llaeniau is a rare but typical example of a building type that was at one time common in Wales – a 'Tŷ Un Nos' or 'One Night House', but by its very nature very few survive today. It is not grand or architecturally magnificent, but is perhaps representative of what is special about Welsh architecture – our vernacular traditions and how they relate to the way we lived many years ago.

Llaeniau started life as one of hundreds of Tŷ Un Nos, or squatters dwellings that popped up like mushrooms all over Wales in the 18th century. They were built by the landless poor who were forced to take the law into their own hands by building homes on common land. A tradition grew that if they could put up four walls and a roof, and get a fire lit inside and smoke rising from the roof by daybreak, they could lay claim to the land. The throwing of an axe marked the distance from the house that you claimed as your land. Of course, these buildings that were thrown up over night weren't built to a very good standard and consequently didn't last very long. Soon after construction many started planning their more permanent home by replacing it with something more durable with stone walls and thatched roofs. These were known as second generation Tŷ Un Nos and that's exactly how our little cottage was derived – Llaeniau is a second generation Tŷ Un Nos.

The building of the original house was essentially a co-operative. It had to be, as a man and wife could not build even the most meagre of cottages in a single night. One group would clear the site and build the walls with clods of turf, and another group would collect timber for the roof trusses.

A modest little house that looks like a cake covered with icing.

The original house sits in the middle of two later additions.

As soon as smoke had risen from the chimney it was deemed that the house could not be pulled down. Once a cottage had been established, a bit more land was added year by year, until a little farm might develop with the house sitting in the middle of its conspicuous cultivated green fields. There was much resentment of the squatters by the farmers who regarded them as lazy. But many were craftsmen – basket makers, weavers, tailors, that had contributed to the rural economy. They also improved numerous acres of waste land and established new housing for the rural poor at no cost to the local government or the Crown. In a seemingly poetic snub to the landed gentry and the resentful farmers, the names given to these squatters dwellings had an ironic tone: Grand Porch, Thimble Court, Bodkin Hall, and The Castle.

But many of these cottage farmhouses were abandoned in the second half of the 19th century with migration to the South Wales coalfields.

The relative luxury of the terraced houses of the Valleys was immeasurably better than the cottages on the commons.

Llaeniau nestles on the side of a hill with only one or two other cottages visible on the other side of the valley. It is a long, low single storey building, and appears rather different to when it was built in the 18th century.

Above left: An early sliding sash window, distinguished by the lack of 'horns' on the corners of the sashes.

Above right: Evan and Daphnine sitting in their favourite spot enjoying the evening sun.

This remote little cottage has been home for Evan and Daphnine for over 33 years. It has been in Evan's family for generations, who farmed the land and worked in the nearby quarry. When Evan's grandmother got old the family moved out of the house and sold it to a local farmer. Evan asked him if he could have first refusal on the property if ever he came to sell.

A couple of years later the farmer wrote to him saying he was ready to sell. The timing wasn't good as they had just bought a house, so they had to go to a loan shark to borrow enough money to secure the little cottage.

Evan and Daphnine remember when they were the youngest in the community and had to drag the milk up from the bottom of the hill for the neighbours who weren't able to do it themselves – now they are the older generation in the community.

The original structure sits in the middle, with two later additions either side. Entering the original cottage in the centre, very little has changed. At one end is a large fireplace with a chimney rising up through the roof, at the other end of the room is a partition that separates the main living room from what was the parlour but is now a small narrow kitchen. Above the end room is a 'crog loft' – which was a small sleeping space in

13

It's quite rare to find this little cottage with its surviving 'crog loft', and still being used as a bedroom.

the loft, accessed only by a steep ladder from the living room. This layout, with two rooms downstairs and a tiny little 'crog loft' at one end, was very common at one time in north west Wales, but they are not suitable for modern living and many have been extended and altered out of all recognition. So it is quite rare to find this little cottage with its surviving 'crog loft', but also because the 'crog loft' is still being used as a bedroom by Evan and Daphnine.

Daphnine says that the loft is cold in winter and hot in the summer, but she loves to lie in bed and hear the wind blowing outside, feeling safe and secure in her cwtsh. It is very cramped for space, like the rest of the cottage, but originally the loft would have slept half a dozen people, and possibly more sleeping down stairs.

As I surveyed the outside of the building with Evan it reminded me of a charming little cake covered with icing. The slates on the roof had been covered with a slurry of mortar to cover all the gaps and keep the rain and snow from blowing in. The roof was undulating up and down along its length, gently blending into the walls and chimneys. Evan had been curious to know what the slabs of stone were sticking out of the chimney. These are 'drip stones', a very traditional detail for protecting the joint between roof and chimney. Although they were quite a distance above the roof I think this was due to the fact that this is not the original roof covering, which would most likely have been thatch, and a lot thicker (and therefore higher up the chimney) than the slates on the roof today.

Either side of the little entrance door there were two simple sliding sash windows, one to light the living room and the other lighting the kitchen. Although these two windows appeared identical I couldn't help notice a subtle difference. One of them had 'horns' and the other did not. This was a telling detail which pointed to their age and history. From this and the narrowness of the glazing bars on the window without 'horns' I was able to confirm that this was the older, and probably the original window, whilst the window with 'horns' and thicker glazing bars was much later.

The earlier window also had a name scratched into the glass – 'William Hughes'. Evan explained that William was his grandfather who was a bit of a character. He must have added his name in the 1920s. Evan, feeling a sense of history, also left his mark, by carving his name and

When you open your door each morning there is a beautiful scene to greet you.

dating it 'Ebrill 14 1954' in the stone door step. But is this graffiti? I often come across all kinds of words, dates and pictures on old buildings. But when is a mark on a building graffiti, and how old does it have to be before it becomes an accepted part of its history?

Llaeniau is a remarkable little building – a piece of history frozen in time. Interestingly, during the break up of the Church in Wales when Welsh people were starting to worship in chapels, the cottage was used as a place of worship, before the chapels were built. My great concern for this cottage is who will come after Evan and Daphnine. When they move on I can't see another couple willing to live the very simple and meagre lifestyle that this cottage demands. The pressure to modernise will be unbearable, and another Tŷ Un Nos will be lost.

Sliding sash windows

Timber sliding sash windows were first introduced into Britain in the 16th century and have been one of the most enduring styles of windows ever seen. They have been through various modifications throughout the centuries but have remained essentially the same. They started with very small panes of glass, but as glass technology improved so the pane sizes increased. At the end of 19th century large panes became very desirable to maximize both the view out and the light coming in. The larger panes were heavy and without all the glazing bars there was less wooden frame work to support them. So, the joint in the bottom corner of the frame was strengthened by overlapping the frame at the corner of the sash.

The projecting piece of timber – a 'horn' – was usually given a decorative design. Horns were not introduced until the 1850s, and much later in some parts of the country.

The window displays a collection of interesting ornaments.

2 Penwhilwr

Two storey straw bale house

According to the fairy story it's not wise to build a house of straw, particularly if you plan on sheltering from the big bad wolf. But nowadays, even in our damp climate, it is one of the most sustainable ways to build. I went to see a most unusual house in St. Dogmaels, Cardiganshire. A 'pink' self-built house set in an acre of terraced woodland overlooking the Teifi Estuary. The house was built by Rachel Whitehead and her partner Ravi – and an army of friends and neighbours.

Overlooking the Teifi Estuary in St Dogmaels, Cardiganshire.

Rachel acquired an ancient ruin, which forms the basis of the straw bale house, in the year 2000. The land is called 'Penwhilwr' – Welsh for a kind of lookout or watch tower. Apparently it was one of the oldest buildings in the village, and is certainly strategically placed for keeping watch over the mouth of the river. She had waited two years to get planning consent to build her sustainable home, during which time she lived in a shed without electricity, carrying water from the local spring, using candlelight, a gas stove and a chemical toilet.

   Rachel says that she had always planned to use ordinary builders, but when you're building something rather special she found they didn't seem to do things the way she wanted, and she soon realised that she would have to do it herself. She gave up her career as a dance teacher so she could live with nature and let the simple daily tasks of living unfold. Rachel recalls "As the season changed, nature spoke to me in her wisdom. I learnt to listen to her voice, breathe in the stillness and surrender as the many obstacles arose... marvelling at the power of nature as I tied down

The combination of straw bales and lime render provide a soft appearance, whilst the straw, solar panels and grass roof give it excellent 'eco' credentials.

The blue Tŷ Nant bottles provide a glowing light at the bottom of the wall – such an imaginative way to recycle.

some plastic on the roof in a hailstorm at midnight in the middle of winter." Rachel spent three years building the house, much of the expertise coming from 'Amazon Nails', an all women building team and the pioneers of straw bale building in Britain.

The house at Penwhilwr is unique as it is the only two storey load bearing straw bale house in Britain. The straw bales directly support the load of the roof and the floors, unlike others that are constructed as a timber frame with the straw bales acting as non load bearing walls. However, a frame was used on the south side where large areas of glazing were needed to capture the warmth of the sun. Placing heavy roofs and floors on to straw bales makes them compress, and some allowance has to be made in the design and construction. Straw as a building material is cheap and has very high insulation values (U-value = 0.13). Energy savings of up to 75% compared with a conventional modern house can be achieved with the use of straw. This form of building however is not a main stream conventional building method and tends to be restricted to the self-builder. And yet it is very simple to build with – its just like laying blocks, and is reassuringly inaccurate. The bales are secured with hazel

Below: A straw bale wall ready for the internal plaster made of clay, sand and manure.

stakes driven through the top of them down into the bale below. It is a natural, breathable material that has no harmful effects, unlike many modern building materials, which are now known to cause long term harm. Once constructed the bales are trimmed to give them an even surface before plastering. Rachel saw the opportunity to be creative with the design of her home by trimming and carving the massive blocks of straw, sculpting them into all kinds of shapes and moulding the plaster to create some interesting and practical effects – there's an elephant, niches, floral patterns and so on. One of the most innovative ideas is the use of the 'Tŷ Nant' water bottles. A curving wall between the main living space and the entrance lobby is built of three rows of the famous blue bottles. The straw bales are simply pressed firmly over the necks of the bottles, creating a blue glass fringe to the soft flowing wall. The light coming in through the window on the other side of the wall makes the bottles gently glow, throwing a blue light over the floor.

The straw bales are covered with a lime plaster externally, and internally with a mixture of refined clay, from a local brickworks, sand,

cow manure and straw. Animal waste, such as manure, has been used in plaster mixes for centuries as it helps to bind the different elements together. Once the recipe is well mixed together it is applied to the wall by pressing it firmly into the straw bales with your hands but, as I found when helping Rachel with a spot of plastering, the surface must be dampened first so that the wall doesn't suck all the moisture out of the clay too quickly. I got a quick telling off from Rachel, who said I was suffering from 'clay fever'. The house is not very big – about the size of an average 4 bedroomed detached house, but the internal plastering, all applied by hand, took Rachel and her little helpers about eight months to complete. No wonder this is not a commercial build and can only be entertained if another form of plastering is adopted internally.

One of the special features of this house is the ground floor bathroom. Rachel wanted to reflect its original use as a tower, so the bathroom is circular. The bath sits in the centre of the room sunk into the floor. This is the one area of the house that has stone walls and these are punctured with more glass bottles of all different colours set within the thickness

The bathroom sits under a grass roof, its rounded shaped reminiscent of the original watchtower that stood on the site.

The living room is separated from the kitchen by a wood burning stove that heats the whole house.

of the wall. As the sun moves around the building, it catches each of the bottles and sends a shaft of light into the room. Although I haven't tried it – imagine relaxing in your bath with coloured circular lights reflected on the wall, ever so slowly moving across the wall tracking the path of the sun. The bathroom is topped off with a turf roof that also acts as a balcony. The balcony extends over the outside terrace and is roofed over with a large piece of bullet-proof glass that Rachel recalls pulling out of a skip outside Lloyds bank. It had been rejected because it had a slight crack in it.

The building is heated by a ceramic wood burning stove and, thanks to the high insulation value of the straw bales this is sufficient to heat the whole house using an underfloor heating system. Power for the house is drawn from a wind turbine and four photovoltaic solar panels mounted on the roof.

Rachel said there were many challenges she had to face building such a unique house on a very special site. Access was very difficult as the site was on a high location up a narrow track, which was also a public footpath. Having to haul large pieces of timber and 350 straw bales up this path

Above left: Finishing touches – a handrail is fashioned from a single branch.
Above right: Rachel relaxes in a cosy corner of her home, surrounded by soft curved walls and little niches.

was very challenging. But friends and neighbours came to the rescue – Susannah, a local tree surgeon friend came with her working mule, Monty. He dragged the timber up to the site over three days, "quietly and gracefully", recalls Rachel.

Now that the house is complete, Rachel feels a great sense of achievement and satisfaction, and what a magnificent place to live. Wouldn't we all love to live in a house that is not only different to any other house, but also built with your own 'fair' hands. And fair hands they were, as many of those involved with the project were women. Rachel sums it up by saying "Working with a group of women is a beautiful and empowering experience. The mystique of building soon dissolved as each stage clearly guided by Barbara Jones (Amazon Nails) became clearer and just made sense. Sometimes I would ring Barbara and say 'I need a plumber...' and she would reply 'Rachel, you can do it yourself. It's just like lego. I'll send you the drawings'. So, it was clear that as much as I tried to pass some of the work on, it became more apparent that if I was to see this vision through, I was going to have to oversee the project and trust I could with the full support of the universe".

Having to haul large pieces of timber and 350 straw bales up this path was very challenging. But friends and neighbours came to the rescue.

Rachel now lives out her dream of living in a sustainable home, whilst making silver jewellery and developing natural essences from flowers and herbs, which she sells on her website – Gwalia Essences. (www.gwaliaessences.com)

The rounded front of the house with a swan moulded into the plaster next to the front door.

3   Rhiwbina Garden Village
A model village built away from the city

Imagine the scenario – a group of businessmen get together and borrow large sums of money, buy a tract of land on the outskirts of the city, and build hundreds of affordable homes for working class people. What's more, they stand no chance of making any profit. How likely is that to happen? Well, in Cardiff in 1912 that's exactly what did happen.

North of Cardiff,
4 miles from the
city centre.

The buildings at Y Groes surround the Village Green which forms the centrepiece of the Garden Village.

At the dawn of the 20th century Britain faced a massive housing problem. Millions of working class families were crammed into appalling slums. This was the case in Cardiff and something had to be done to improve working class housing. The answer? – A Garden Village.

Inspired by Letchworth and Hamstead Garden Cities, a Cardiff professor of economics called Stanley Jevons formed a Housing Reform Company in 1911 to build a Garden Village for the working classes on the outskirts of the city. Their aim was to create a model village, built away from the city, providing space, gardens, trees, open streets, and good health. They purchased ten acres of land north of Cardiff, and by July 1913 had completed the first 32 houses that were to become Rhiwbina Garden Village. Today, the Garden Village remains virtually unchanged. The trees and hedges have grown, and there are a lot more vehicles, but the houses and village are still the same.

The Garden Village was to be run on co-operative lines. No resident was to own the house they lived in. Instead, each resident took out shares in the company that managed the Garden Village and could have their say. Living in a Garden Village didn't come without its rules. Tenants had to keep their houses in pristine order. For example, if you took a picture rail down, you

RHUBINA FIELDS
CARDIFF WORKER'S CO-OPERATIVE
GARDEN VILLAGE SOCIETY
LIMITED.

"Health for the Child"

Rail from Rhymney Station
Motor Bus from North Road.

Above left: White roughcast render, slate roofs, tall chimneys, and little canopies over the front doors are typical features of the village.
Above right: Front cover of the sales booklet, showing how idyllic life could be if you lived in Rhubina Fields.

had to store it, so that when you left you could fix it back up again. All the houses had to be painted in the Village colours – windows and doors were 'Buckingham Green'. If you did happen to use the wrong colours you were told to change them. The rules, displayed in the rent book, were written by the tenants themselves who were, after all, shareholders and their own bosses. Some examples of the rules were:

• Keep in good order all garden ground, lawns, paths, hedges. No tenant shall cut down, lop, damage, destroy or remove any tree or adjoining fence.
• Use of premises – No trade to be carried out in the house. No notice board, sign board, business plate or advertisement shall be exhibited. The conduct of the tenant shall not be detrimental to good neighbourship.
• Disposal of Refuse – Garden refuse must not be deposited on any vacant land or open space on the estate.
• Wireless – Tenants are required to exercise reasonable discretion in the use of wireless sets, particularly in the summer months.

The Garden Village created the perfect community environment, a wonderful place to bring up a young family. Sylvia Morgan has lived in Y Groes all her life. She was born at number 13 in 1921. "I remember

Everyone turned out for the celebrations and parties on the Village Green.

we all came out to play on the Village Green. We had a Maypole on May 1st, weather permitting, and a Carnival Queen. If there were any royal celebrations we had a party on the Green. You realised that this was different to anywhere else".

Rhiwbina Garden Village was an idyllic place to live, as Julia Hitchings remembers: "Going to Cardiff was a big event as it was well away from Rhiwbina. Coming home, it seemed we were right out in the country, away from civilisation, which was lovely".

Architecturally, Rhiwbina Garden Village was a revolution in Wales. Each house was self contained with its own garden, electric light, gas, and flushing indoor toilets. The houses were built with the latest 'cavity wall' construction, and there were no back extensions to block out the light. There was a bath and hot water in every house, cupboards, and a patent Interoven Stove in each front room – a revolution at the time. Rhiwbina Garden Village today is one of the most sought after places to live in Cardiff. So, you can imagine how it must have felt to be offered a house in such an idyllic location in 1913. The houses cost between £242 and £353 to build for the original 32 houses, and rents were between £28 and £45 per year.

Above left: A collection of gables and a doorway framed by an arched hedge.
Above right: The 'Wendy House' was, and still is, the nerve centre of village life.

The designs were based upon the 'arts and crafts' movement with roughcast render, small thick slates, steeply pitched gables, tall chimneys, and wide eaves. They had symmetrical windows with small panes that give a sense of well planned unity to the village as a whole. But there is also variety. Some are built in terraces whilst others are semi-detached, and some in small groups. As you enter the Village Green at Y Groes, you notice the long terrace opposite. Although a terrace, it appears to have been conceived as one large country house, giving a grand appearance overlooking a spacious green. Deception maybe, but this was part of the overall concept of taking the working classes out of the dark slums of the city and presenting them with a dream scenario.

Sitting inconspicuously, tucked away in a corner of the Village Green is the affectionately named 'Wendy House'. This was originally the site office whilst the houses were being constructed. Thereafter it became the nerve centre of village life, and still performs a community function today.

Below: Traditional building styles with an abundance of trees and hedges, provide a picturesque setting.

It was here that the rent was collected, and requests for maintenance or any problems were reported. Mary Clarke, the current Garden Village Association Chairwoman recalls how her father was the 'works foreman' and had a little group of men working for him. "If you had a problem it would be reported at the little office and if it couldn't be fixed with a nail, a piece a wood or a lump of putty it wasn't going to be fixed". Jeff Heath is Mary's brother and he joined his father's maintenance team when he was only 15 years old. He recalls, "On the way to work I used to cycle from Llanishen with my dad. My first job was to go into the newsagents and buy 40 Woodbines and hand them over to him. Even today when I'm working at some of the houses in the Garden Village; in peoples attics; behind bath panels; under floor boards, I still find old Woodbine packets, and it hits me – My Dad!"

But the social utopian vision was doomed to fail. The ambitious ideas of the Company with low density cottage design houses, meant that the rent they had to charge just to cover their costs was, in reality, too expensive for the average working class family. Instead, the married children of the

A variety of gables and covered porches face onto the main avenue, Lon Y Dail.

Society members were given first call on renting the houses – not what was originally intended.

The timing of their venture wasn't good either, with the development commencing just a few years before the outbreak of the First World War. Consequently, the Housing Reform Company ran into financial difficulty and had to be wound up. The Welsh Town Planning and Housing Trust took over the project, and by the end of 1915 the Rhiwbina Garden Village Limited owned 52 houses. Problems continued throughout the decades with the site being simply too expensive to run as a housing co-operative. In 1968 a meeting was held and the tenant shareholders were offered the leasehold on their houses at a very low cost. Sylvia Morgan was at the meeting and remembers the houses being offered for £300 each. Someone stood up and said 'don't you mean £3,000'. The committee confirmed that they were being offered at £300. The residents couldn't believe it, and they were all sold. The tenants were of course delighted.

So, was the Rhiwbina Garden Village a success? Architecturally there is no doubting its success. However, the vision of providing the working classes with hundreds of houses and a network of shops and amenities did not materialise. Building so many houses to such high standards

Below: Dappled sunlight casts evocative shadows onto the white rendered walls.

at a cost affordable to an average working class family just wasn't possible. The costs of maintenance and co-operative ownership proved unrealistic. Today, it has become one of the most desirable places to live in Cardiff, with house prices in excess of £300,000. It is now designated a Conservation Area and is therefore protected by the Welsh Assembly Government.

It is quite astonishing what the Rhiwbina Garden Village Company had achieved over a 50 year period. They had managed to build 189 houses through two world wars, and with no subsidies from government or local authority. Everyone who invested in the Company was repaid in full with enough over to make a small donation to charity. Walking through the Village today the idyllic intentions of Jevons is clearly evident. The combination of pretty cottages surrounded by trees, hedges and open spaces provides a sense of peacefulness that is scarcely found in modern developments.

Garden Cities

The Garden Cities movement was pioneered by Ebenezer Howard in 1899, an inventor of shorthand typing machines. In 1902 he published his famous book 'Garden Cities of Tomorrow'. It was a reaction against the worst effects of urbanisation caused by the Industrial Revolution and the ever increasing population of inner city slums – referred to by some as 'the cities of dreadful night'. The Garden City concept was quite radical as it addressed issues of sustainability, social equality and co-operative ownership of resources.

At the heart of the Garden City would be a formalised town centre, shaped round wide public boulevards and parks. Housing would be grouped informally down wide streets that were often curved, around village greens and squares, attempting to emulate the organic and settled feel of the medieval village. Eighty percent of the town's area would be given to natural and landscaped green space, with industry located on the edge of the town boundary linked to wider markets by electric train, reducing pollution and ensuring clean air. The first Garden Cities were in Letchworth, and Hampstead Garden Suburb outside London, both designed by Barry Parker and Raymond Unwin. It was their practice that was responsible for Rhiwbina. Houses were based upon the traditional cottage style, clear, simple and unpretentious. Today's suburbs owe much to the Garden City movement and had a huge influence on the way cities expanded and grew.

The Garden City concept was quite radical as it addressed issues of sustainability, social equality and co-operative ownership of resources.

A covered seating area between two houses, divided by a simple round column.

4

West Usk Lighthouse
A guiding light through troubled waters

The Severn Estuary has the second biggest tide in the world and is one of the most treacherous stretches of water in the UK. But on a misty September morning we found ourselves braving the currents and clambering into a small boat to approach the Lighthouse from the water.

At the junction of the Severn and the Usk Estuary, overlooking the Bristol Channel.

Left: Lamp room topped off with a directional weather vein.
Above: The Sheahan family enjoying the view.

It really is the best way of seeing this building for the first time, just as the ships would have when they passed by nearly two hundred years ago. Although no longer a lighthouse, you can spend a night in this unique Bed & Breakfast with a difference – and what a difference!

West Usk Lighthouse in Wentlooge near Newport, was built in 1821 by the renowned Scottish lighthouse engineer, James Walker. He was responsible for many of Britain's most famous lighthouses, such as Bishop's Rock in the Isles of Scilly and Wolf rock which lies 8 miles off Lands End.

He built 26 in all, but this was his first, and that makes it very special. For 101 years the West Usk Lighthouse guided ships up the estuary until it

WEST USK LIGHTHOUSE

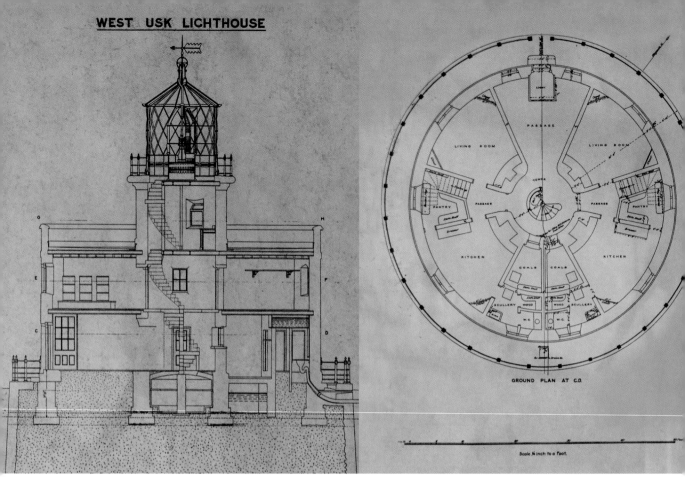

GROUND PLAN AT C.D.

Scale ¼ inch to a Foot.

Original drawings of the lighthouse. The section shows the spiral stairs leading up to the lamp room; and the plan shows how the lighthouse was designed to accommodate two families.

was decommissioned in 1922. In 1987 it was rescued by the Sheahan family who made it their home and an unusual Bed & Breakfast.

Frank Sheahan is passionate about lighthouses. He gave me a tour of this slightly odd lighthouse – the first thing you notice is its rather squat shape. Rather than being a tall elegant tower that you normally associate with this building type, it has a broad cylindrical drum around its base. Frank thinks this was an engineering solution to building on such soft boggy ground, spreading its load over a larger area. As we mulled over the original plans of the building I noticed that there appeared to be two of everything – two living rooms, two kitchens etc... The plan was very symmetrical, so that as you entered the building through the front door, whatever was on the left of the entrance hall was also on the right. Frank explained that this was because the Lighthouse was occupied by two Keepers and their families. There was the Principal Keeper – the PK, and the Assistant Keeper – the AK. This is quite different to how I imagined it would be. I pictured two lonely keepers sharing an isolated life, cut off from civilisation.

As an old photograph confirmed, this was in fact a little community of two households, sharing a busy life manning the lighthouse. Although the

USK LIGHTHOUSE 1879

Photograph taken in 1879 of the principal keeper and his assistant with their families.

Lighthouse is now surrounded by land and sitting on the edge of the river, it was originally totally surrounded by water, cut off from the land, until the tide went out to expose a small causeway. This was the only contact with land and a chance for provisions to be brought up to the Lighthouse. The plan of the building shows how the rooms are neatly arranged around a central spiral stairs rising up the full height of the building to the lamp room. Rooms are unusually wedge shaped like segments of a cake, creating interesting spaces, but difficult to furnish.

The central stairs have a significance all of their own. I think it's the combination of being a direct route to the Lamp Room and also being the absolute centre of this round building. It is the hub of the whole operation. The spine upon which everything else is built. Just imagine how many times those steps have been trodden by the Keepers, making sure the ships are kept safe in these treacherous waters. Its significance hasn't escaped Frank's sense of humour either, as he has labelled it 'The Stairway to Heaven'. Not surprising as, when you get to the top, you are surrounded by windows with wonderful views over the night sky. Just below floor level, surrounding the base of the stairs, is a freshwater chamber where water is drawn from the roof through lead-lined channels and stored

Above: A typical bedroom in the lighthouse.
Right: 'Stairway to Heaven' rising up through the centre of the lighthouse.

as the only freshwater available to the Keepers and their families. There maybe some lessons to be learnt here. We are currently growing more conscious of the need to conserve water – we are now starting to collect 'grey' water for flushing toilets and washing clothes. There is a lot we can learn from the past – even a 200 year old lighthouse.

Danielle Sheahan recalls going through the Exchange & Mart and coming across a short advert saying 'Lighthouse for sale. £80,000' They got in the car the very next day to view the building. It was semi-derelict. The Lamp Room didn't exist and there were cows and sheep roaming through it. The thing that really appealed to them both was how quiet it was. They stood on the roof and couldn't hear a thing, only the cows munching in the fields below. "Coming from London this was quite amazing", says Frank. "It was the quietness of the place".

Left: The Lamp Room
at the top of the
Lighthouse.
Above: West Usk
Lighthouse set on the
Severn Estuary.

On the outside of the Lighthouse there are very few clues to its eccentric and captivating interior. The Hall is quite bright and well lit, and is full of odd objects like a large fish tank; a stuffed seagull suspended from the ceiling; and an old sign that says 'Steam Ferry Landing'. Sitting in the corner is a wooden telephone box from an old ship that sank. This is not the only telephone box in the building. There's a white box just outside, and a red one in their son's bedroom. This is a clue to another of Frank's obsessions – Dr Who.

At the base of the stairs sits one of only three original Daleks to survive. One assumes the others were all annihilated by The Doctor! Of the other two Frank says that one is in a private collection, and the other in a museum. "They were defeated from taking over the world because they couldn't get up the stairs. So, it's quite appropriate it's here in a lighthouse, sitting at the bottom of the spiral stairs." Frank has plans to build a TARDIS on the roof and then convert it into a shower. The crowning glory and function of any lighthouse is its Lamp Room. It's from here that the all important signal is sent out to ships so they can safely plot their course and avoid crashing into land. But the one here didn't exist when they started the renovations, as it was all boxed in with asbestos. As you enter the room, surrounded by glass, you can feel the increased temperature as the sun heats up the space. However, the vertical glazing bars were not good for the proper functioning of a lighthouse. As the light radiated out around the top of the building, the signal was constantly broken up by the vertical bars. So, in about 1856 they redesigned the lanterns by replacing the vertical bars with a slim diamond pattern. When Frank and Danielle bought the Lighthouse the Lamp Room was missing, and so they set about rebuilding it from the little information they could find. They appear to have made a really good job of it – after all, a lighthouse would not be a lighthouse without its Lamp Room. It really makes the building complete.

The real magic of this place is the combination of living in a converted lighthouse, and the eccentric way that Frank and Danielle have decorated the building.

Frank and Danielle strongly believe in 'spirituality' and offer all kinds of therapies for their guests, the most popular being aromatherapy and reflexology. They seem to have a different outlook on life, and claim that it's living near the sea in such an unusual building that nurtures these feelings. Danielle says "We enjoy living near the water. Everyday is different. It's beautiful seeing the sea coming in and going out. The colour is changing all the time. When it's a clear night with a full moon and the tide is in, we can sit on the roof in the hot tub, with a glass of wine and watch the stars. Now that's pretty special".

Frank says that although the lighthouse is quiet and remote, there's always something happening. He recalls when there was a knock at the door early in the morning. A man said that a whale had been washed up on the beach. "I ran up to the roof and could see the huge mammal through my telescope. It was a privilege to see the 61ft, 40 ton beast, but was terribly sad as well. Living here has made some days very exciting. It's certainly different from London".

The real magic of this place is the combination of living in a converted lighthouse, and the eccentric way that Frank and Danielle have decorated the building. The Lighthouse is full of unusual objects – model lighthouses, ships, stuffed birds, telephone boxes, a Dalek…. So, if you want to get away from it all and have a short, but unusual break, then why not try visiting a lighthouse on the South Wales coast. (www.westusklighthouse.co.uk)

Above left: A view out to see from one of the bedrooms.
Above right: A nautical compass set into the front door below the knocker.

Lighthouses

The origins of the lighthouse are not definitively known. Families with loved ones at sea would place a light in the windows of their homes to help guide them back safely. A light placed in a prominent position such as a roof or the top of a tower would be much more visible, and this practice was generally adopted.

Before clearly defined ports were developed, mariners were also guided by fires built on hilltops. As the fires would be more easily visible if they were raised, they began to be built on platforms. This was one of the practices that led to the development of the lighthouse. The French use the word 'Phare' to describe a lighthouse. The word is derived from the ancient light tower at Pharos near Alexandria. (3rd century B.C.) Germans use the word 'Leuchtturme', or light tower.

New developments in navigational aids – such as Global Positioning Satellite (GPS) are threatening the future of lighthouses. There are now less than 1,500 operational lighthouses worldwide.

5 The Georgian houses of Tenby

Elegance and style at the seaside

If you were asked to think of a Welsh holiday town by the sea you are more than likely to picture the beautiful scene overlooking the harbour at Tenby, with its sandy North Beach sweeping into the protected harbour, surrounded by layers of colourful Regency architecture.

Located in Pembrokeshire National Park.

Contrasting styles at the rear of Rock Terrace facing the sea.
The slate hung walls provide protection from the severe coastal weather.
Pages 48/49: Aerial view of Tenby.

This is one of the most popular tourist destinations in Wales, and there's probably nowhere more picturesque in Britain. But it hasn't always been so grand. Over the years Tenby has been visited by the Vikings, it's been invaded by the Normans, and in the Middles Ages it was one of the busiest sea ports in Wales.

Wealthy merchants had lived in Tenby since the 13th century and the town had grown big and prosperous, and so had its buildings. In fact Tenby was well known for being finely built in medieval times. But then, in the 17th century Tenby was hit by war and plague. Firstly the Civil War devastated the town's trade, and soon after the population was wiped out by an outbreak of the plague. Consequently, the core of the town was completely deserted and left to fall into ruin. Tom Lloyd tells us how there were pigs running through the streets, because there was nobody living there.

The pigs were feeding in the deserted back gardens. The only building to survive this period intact is the Tudor Merchant's House, and some stone barrel-vaulted cellars hidden under later Victorian buildings.

The 18th century was much kinder to Tenby. It was a time when people became much more interested in discovering their own country as the Napoleonic wars severely restricted people's movement around the continent. As a result, tourism improved considerably in Wales and

Colourful Georgian terraces surround Tenby harbour.

Scotland. Sea bathing became the popular and healthy pastime, and people came streaming down to Tenby to bathe at the two magnificent beaches, enjoy its vitality, freshness and abundant nature. Such a popular resort attracted the speculators who built hotels, restaurants, inns, and lots of houses. This redevelopment of Tenby all happened rather quickly around 1800, and nothing much has changed to this day. One of the architectural gems of Tenby is hidden down at the harbour. Tom Lloyd describes it as "The crowning achievement of Georgian Tenby – a highly sophisticated tourist attraction". The Bathhouse was built by Sir William Paxton and designed by S. P. Cockerell providing hot and cold swimming baths for the tourists. It used the salt water from the sea, that came in and out on the tides, providing a constant source of clean fresh water. But the key attraction was that it had a 'hot' bath, heated by a huge furnace so that you didn't need to get cold bathing in the cold sea waters. This was such a novelty and attracted huge numbers.

Paxton's own house is situated on the south side of Tudor Square in the centre of the town. He developed his house in 1802, out of an old coaching-inn known as the Globe Inn, after his return from India where he made his fortune. The building, now the Tenby House Hotel, has three storeys with a

painted stuccoed façade and a typical Regency style canopied balcony.

Castle Square presents the picture postcard view and backdrop to Tenby
harbour, the steep topography adding to the dramatic composition.
The modest cottages on the front give way to tall narrow façades that make
up St Julian's Terrace, each one slightly different to the next – some attic
floors are in the roof whilst others are placed within the stucco façade;
the door cases vary from round head to square, some with pitched roof
canopies and one has a balcony extending across its entire front.
This variety in height, colour, and detail breaks up the formality of the
group whilst still maintaining its cohesion as a Regency terrace.

Further south west along St Julian's Street is Lexden Terrace, probably the finest row of Georgian houses in Tenby.

Further south west along St Julian's Street is Lexden Terrace, probably
the finest row of Georgian houses in Tenby, a much more sober and
dominating group of buildings. It was built by a local builder, Mr Smith,
for Captain John Rees. They began with No.1 in 1843 and completed the

Left: Lexden terrace, one of the first Georgian terraces to be built in Tenby. Number one is at the far end with the projecting porch.
Below left: A typical Georgian door case in Rock Terrace.
Below right: Imposing entrance off St. Julian's Street.

terrace with Lexden House where Mr Smith decided to take up residence. On approaching the house you feel the gently imposing sophistication of this Georgian house, and yet only three out of the five floors are visible. Such was the social character of this period that the carefully designed façade ensured that the servants were tucked away out of sight. The attic floor, or Garrett, is set back behind the parapet, and the basement floor, although having windows to the front, are neatly placed below ground level. The architecture of status continues with the ground floor windows being tallest, the first floor smaller and the second floor smaller again – a centuries old classical hierarchy. Censuses of 1881 and 1891 confirm that the household was attended by four live-in servants. Each house in the terrace is divided from the next by a series of giant ionic pilasters on the front façade, and the developer, wanting to distinguish his house from the rest, built Lexden House slightly wider and added an ionic portico. Sadly the main façade was spoiled when bathrooms were introduced inside and the necessary soil pipes tacked on to the main face of the terrace.

The Regency terraces continue along St Julian's Street, built around

1830. Nos. 1 - 2 Rock Houses have giant ionic pilasters with heavily corniced parapets. Nos. 3 - 4 are set back behind railed gardens, with a rusticated front and a pair of panelled doors with fanlights and trellised porch. In total contrast, the rear sea facing side of Rock Terrace is covered with slate hanging, a local tradition to protect the façade from the prevailing weather. It looks rather odd to see the elegance of the Georgian sash windows set into a slate hung façade, a combination you don't see every day – unless you live in Tenby of course.

As you walk around the town you can spot the Regency details of Georgian architecture if you look carefully. The Georgian buildings are in the prime locations, near the sea, as that's where they started developing first.

One way is to look for the genuine Georgian sash windows – these are the ones with the delicately thin glazing bars, and the absence of 'horns' on the corner of the sashes. I'm happy to say that there are still many to be found, and when you think that most of these are nearly two hundred years old, there is a compelling argument to use good quality timber windows in our houses today.

Nos 3 - 4 Rock terrace set back off the street. The doors are framed with a delicate trellised porch.

A view down
St. Julian's Street.

The Georgian Terrace.
There are three general periods of Georgian architecture that span
throughout the 18th century and into the 19th. Early Georgian (1714-1765),
late Georgian (1765-1811), and Regency (1811-1837). The Georgian style
is based on the Classical influences of ancient Rome, and the writings of
Italian architect Andreas Palladio. These include uniformity, proportion,
grace, and the use of the Classical 'orders' of architecture. Designs were
set out to a strict pattern, firstly designed by the influential architects of
the day such as William Kent, and then later Robert Adam and John Soane,
but then copied by the speculative developers who produced buildings from
pattern books. The Georgian terrace is probably Britain's most successful
building type. These terraces were given a sense of wholeness, whilst
keeping the size of the houses small. Most terraces were four storeys high,
containing sliding sash windows with thin delicate glazing bars.
Front doors were panelled and often with a semi-circular fanlight above,
and accessed up a short flight of steps.

6

Hafod Y Garreg
The oldest house in Wales

Nestled in a valley amongst the trees a few miles north of Brecon is a special little house in Welsh history. From the outside, this house gives very few clues to its medieval past but the inside is a different story. John Marchant and Annie Mckay moved here from London in 2002 where they were both in the antiques trade. When they started investigating their house they realised it may have a hidden history.

Located a few miles north of Brecon.

The deeds started with the words '*In the year of Philip of Spain 1633...*'. They knew that was quite old, but when they were working on the house they noticed that the main fireplace, with its huge oak beam, had probably been inserted later. The house must have been older than the fireplace.

The main room on the ground floor is full of historic features and has a mellow evocative atmosphere with oak beams and antique pieces of Welsh furniture. As you enter the corner of the room there is a huge 17th century stone fireplace at the right hand side of the room. The fireplace has a deep oak beam over the opening showing all the scars and markings of its past. Two large holes run right through the thickness of the beam, where oak pegs probably once supported a wooden shelf. There are burn marks from candles or rushes, and other deeper blackened scars. These scars may have been made from centuries of wiping ash off a hot poker, buried in the fire before plunging into a tankard of mead to warm it up on a cold winters day. Tucked away at the back of the hearth is a small square recess in the stonework. This is an old salt box for storing what was, then, a valuable commodity, keeping it dry and out of reach of vermin.

A rustic charm welcomes the visitor to Hafod Y Garreg.

The small group of farm buildings nestle in the countryside.

At the left hand side of the room is an early plank and post oak screen. Near the base of the screen there are a series of peg poles, evidence from where a bench was fixed along the length of the screen. These small holes say so much about the original use of this room. For this room would have been a Hall, with the screen and bench at the 'higher' end of the Hall. The room predated the fireplace, as John suspected. Originally, the room would have been larger, extending from the oak screen on the left, to the other side of the stone fireplace. There would be no low ceiling with oak beams, as the room would have extended up to the roof timbers, and the hearth would have been in the centre of the room, rather like a camp fire. Instead of glass in the windows, there would have been sliding wooden shutters to keep the wind and rain out, but also blocked out the light.

The key to the age of this house lies in a single oak truss in one of the bedrooms upstairs. John and Annie sought help from Richard Suggett of

The unassuming appearance of the exterior disguises the layers of history that lie within.

the Royal Commission on Ancient and Historic Monuments in Wales. I have worked many times with Richard who has an enormous knowledge of historic buildings in Wales, and we occasionally swap information about buildings I am working on. He has always encouraged me, where appropriate, to use dendrochronology to try and accurately date buildings and their features. So, I wasn't surprised that he had brought in dendrochronologist Michael Worthington to help unravel the history of this unique little house. The truss at the centre of the investigation is magnificent. The only surviving 'cruck frame' left in the building, or at least the only one visible; others may be buried in later building work.

A cruck frame is where the oak frame of the building forms the structure of the wall and the roof in one piece of timber. This piece of timber is carefully selected from trees in the forest so that it has the right bend to make the shape required for the house. It is then carefully split

The cruck frame that makes this house the oldest in Wales.

Above: The main living room that was originally the Hall, which was open to the roof, and had a hearth in the middle of the floor.
Below: John Marchant and Annie Mckay.

down the middle and two pieces are opened out to create a symmetrical shape – vertical from floor to eaves, and gently bending to form the slope of the roof up to the ridge. To make it more rigid, other pieces of timber are inserted into the trusses, like a collar, or tie beam, running horizontally between the two crucks. The truss at Hafod y Garreg also has deep arched bracing below the collar, as well as a vertical post and further bracing, all lightly decorated with cusps and chamfers. Although the truss has been cut through to insert a door it is nevertheless a truss befitting its status as the oldest in Wales. It was fortunate that the truss had some good timber for sampling. One section contained scars of where its original bark had been – the last remnants of growth. Therefore the dendrochronology was able to reveal that the tree, from which this truss was made, was felled in the summer of 1402. The accuracy of this date was backed up by the other timbers in the house that were all assembled at the same time, so no timbers were reused from another building, which can often be deceiving when try to date old buildings.

Left: A large fireplace filled with logs ready for winter.

Above left: Centuries of marks on the old oak beam across the fireplace.

Above right: The spiral stone stairs wrapping around the back of the fireplace.

Typical of the period, there are stone stairs wrapping around the back of the fireplace, and the oak door frame leading into the living room provides some more interesting details about this house. The doorway is very low with a shallow arched head. In its centre is evidence of a missing piece of decorative timber. I can just imagine how many heads must have struck that piece of wood as they went up and down the steps. So was it removed by collision, or by impatience? Although the oak frame and stonework surrounding are now exposed, the ends of the oak lintel, where it is built into the stonework, has markings made by an adze – an old form of axe. The adze would prick up the surface of the oak, creating a key to help plaster stick to the wood. Therefore, the whole stonework, including part of the oak door frame was covered with plaster, and then limewashed – a different appearance to how we often imagine stone buildings would have looked.

So why has such an early building survived and who built it in the first place? Well, 1402 was a period of great anxiety in Wales. In the summer, exactly when the trees were being felled to build this house, the battle of Pilleth took place, one of the most important battles in Welsh history, where Owain Glyndŵr defeated the English forces of

The dining room provides a fitting atmosphere for a medieval feast.

Left: The living room window looks out to the courtyard and barn beyond.
Above: The landing doubles up as a small sitting room.

Edmund Mortimer, Lord of the March. Richard Suggett believes that the house was constructed directly after the battle, as the Lordship of Brecon wanted to show it was business as usual; and why not. After all, he was the King of England – Henry IV. Richard believes it's a forester's house, but also a hunting lodge for the King, hence its high status.

In subsequent years the timber framed house was significantly modernised and made into a robust stone building, with nearly all of the original timber building buried in the alterations. Externally the house takes on a late 18th century appearance when there was a major re-planning of the house. The entry was moved to its present position next to the oak screen, new windows were inserted, a new timber stair was added and the stone one blocked up, and the roof was raised to provide full height rooms on the upper floors. There is also a barn and other outbuildings set at a slightly splayed angle providing a sheltered enclosure to the front of the house.

Annie has a romantic vision of life in the house, now run as a Bed & Breakfast establishment. She imagines how it must have been, in an apparent oasis protected from the mayhem of plunder and destruction all around; the lovely smell of the logs burning in the hearth, with a hog

67

roasting on the spit. The barn on the other side of the courtyard was a cider mill, and hops were found growing in the hedgerows, so they must have made their own cider and beer. Annie likes to think of people drinking, bards and minstrels playing; the sound of the harp, singing and poetry; visitors coming and going and people having a lovely time. The way the house looks and feels today, it's not difficult to imagine Annie's vision. With a peaceful and secluded location in a wooded valley, a log fire and candles providing the only light, who wouldn't love to spend a night or two in such historic surroundings. (www.hafodygarreg.co.uk)

Dendrochronology

Commonly known as tree ring dating, dendrochronology is the science of dating timbers through tree ring growth. It began being used at the beginning of the 20th century and was discovered by A. E. Douglas of Arizona University. Each year a tree adds a layer of new wood to its trunks and branches. During wet years the tree would grow more, and therefore produce a wider tree ring than in dry years when the tree ring is narrower.

When a sample is taken from a tree, using a boring tool, its ring pattern is studied for matches against trees with known sequences of growth. If you can obtain a sample through the sap wood – last year of growth, then you can determine when the tree was felled, and therefore the date of construction of that element of the building, and possibly the building itself. The process requires a good sample from the timber, normally more than 75 rings, and ideally 100, To be confident of accurate results six to eight samples should be taken to corroborate the results. A 10mm core is drawn from the timber, carefully sawn in half along its length, and sanded to make the rings stand out and their boundaries clearly distinguished. Each ring is then measured and the data entered into a computer program. Analysis and matching with known dated samples usually produces a date for the timber.

An eclectic arrangement of furniture in the living room.

7 Cynefin
A sense of place that nourishes the soul

We have all dreamed about building our own home. To find that piece of land with wonderful views over the Welsh countryside; to create a home that is special, something different; a place where we can happily live out the rest of our days. But to go further, to create a building so in harmony with its surroundings that it feels as if it has its own soul, is more than a dream. Yet, entrepreneur Peter Saunders and his wife Judith have done just that.

In the village of Llanegryn, near Tywyn, in the Snowdonia National Park.

The hand crafted staircase, with the handrail made from a single branch of Welsh ash.

As you walk through their home, the building generates a sense of wellbeing. It feels special, the same sort of feeling you get when you enter an ancient church. It exudes peace.

This stone and slate building lies within the Snowdonia National Park, just outside the village of Llanegryn, near Tywyn. The site is perfectly placed amidst the rolling landscape and against the dramatic backdrop of the two mountain ranges that form the Dysynni Valley – and a rocky crag known as Bird Rock. Many thousands of years ago the sea reached inland to the base of this rock and cormorants made it their nesting place. Although the sea has long since retreated, the birds still venture to Bird Rock to rear their young, making it the furthest inland nesting site of cormorants anywhere in Europe.

When Peter and Judith moved from their conventional home they knew they wanted to build a family home with a blend of the modern and traditional. What better place to create a unique home.

They turned to architects Christopher Day and Julian Bishop, who believe that a building should have a spirit, a soul, and a sense of place.

The roof lines up
perfectly with the
mountains beyond, such
was the thought that
went into its design.

The house is set in beautifully landscaped gardens.

I asked Christopher and Julian to explain their philosophy and how it could be achieved. They explained that places affect how we feel and how we act. As we probably spend most of our lives in buildings, they provide a very important environment for us. Our surroundings are the most important art form we can experience in our lives and therefore they should be handled in that spirit, rather than as a purely utilitarian product. We shop in a 'tin shed' supermarket; we work in the 'tin shed' factory; we holiday in hotels that all look the same and could be anywhere on the planet; and we live on monotonous estates where the houses are ubiquitous little boxes that say nothing about the place. When we see buildings that have been carefully and thoughtfully designed, we respond very differently.

They have a positive impact on our lives. But can these same principles apply to a more modest home? Christopher believes they can. 'Light is free'. It's about creating the right spaces and providing windows that allow the light to penetrate the building.

After careful thought, inspired design, and three years hard work by craftsmen and builders, their vision for Cynefin was finally completed in 2003. The result is a building that is rooted in the landscape, to the extent that, when viewed from the north west, the roof perfectly follows the contours of the mountains beyond. Such is the care that went into the design. The stone walls are strong and extend out into the landscape; the slate roof is angular and undulates, capturing the rainwater and diverting it down to the ground where pools collect it for recycling. With such an unconventional roof, the wooden windows also find themselves bending to angular forms under the sloping roof. Wood, stone and slate all used in an innovative way to create a carefully crafted building – the traditional materials combining nicely with the contemporary forms.

Peter delighted in talking about some of his favourite aspects of the house. He showed me a rounded stone buttress that splayed at the bottom. He said its strong shape was reminiscent of Castell Y Bere in the hills nearby. Although Cynefin is very much a building of its time, it is nevertheless rooted in the past. It has a sense of belonging, a sense of permanence. You can clearly see that much of the stone has been recycled from other buildings, with the white wash still evident in patches, providing a softness to the hard stone. Peter also explained how water plays an

The roofs and walls of the house seem to grow out of the landscape.

The carpentry took two years to complete and every detail has been carefully crafted.

important part in the ambience of the house. When it rains, the water flows down the roof and is guided towards the stone buttresses and down into the water system, where it is pumped around again to create that constant sound of running water. Under the courtyard there are tanks of rainwater that act as a reservoir for the system. The water is used extensively, with little streams and pools running around the house. At the bottom of the garden is a more natural pond with reeds and plants for wildlife. This recycling of stone and water satisfies Peter and Judith's desire to take an environmentally conscious approach to building their home.

But, for me, the real joy was inside where the free flowing forms of the building are reminiscent of Antonio Gaudi's work in Barcelona. The walls are covered with lime plaster in a way that really does justice to this wonderful material; softly flowing around the walls and ceilings. All corners have been softened with rounded edges, the wooden skirtings have been crafted to the curve of the walls, even on the tightest of angles. There are no rectangular doors here – they all seem to bend and sway with the building, taking the shape that is appropriate for that space. Another craftsman, Bill Swann, works in glass and made the beautiful glass panels for the doors. They are decorated with square jewels of lead

A hand made letter box built into the stone wall.

crystal in a variety of natural colours. When the light shines through the glass it projects colourful images on the walls. The craftsmanship is beautiful. The woodwork alone took two years to complete and was all handcrafted from locally sourced oak, ash and yew. The carpenter, Dafydd Davies-Hughes, also crafted one of the main features of the house – the stairs. The handrail is made from a single branch of Welsh ash and as it winds and twists its way from top to bottom, you can feel every natural curve, bump and knot. You can't help but caress the handrail as you walk down the stairs, your hand glides effortlessly over it, as you make that subconscious connection with nature.

Every room you enter is different. There is a surprise around every corner; and yet it all feels right, one space flows into the next. You feel quite happy spending time in any part of the house, including corridors and halls. That's the magic of the place. I suppose, with its arches and curves, it has a cave-like quality, and maybe there is a subliminal link to our primeval past. When you bring art and craft into a house it evokes a feeling of the soul, something deep inside; maybe so deep that we cannot really comprehend it. One of the key successes to good design is natural light; and that's in abundance in this inspiring house. When you walk from the

Left: The different textures and surfaces create interest in all parts of the building. Above: A variety of crafts and artwork adorn the landscaped grounds.

kitchen to the dining space, down some steps and into the living area, you are on a procession through the building. The large windows that surround the living room provide a quality of light and view to the countryside that nourishes the soul. And as I sat in a comfortable chair and looked out of the window at the stunning views, I spied the dramatic Bird Rock in the distance, the windows framing the view. What price for such a picture?

The best way to sum up this building is as Jane Harvey my co-presenter said: "You drive around Wales and see buildings that are frankly a blot on the landscape. But this house is worthy of its surroundings".
Worthy indeed. That is some compliment given the surroundings.
What Peter and Judith have done is to offer patronage to art and architecture, something we see very little of today. They have gone much further than most and created something sculptural in the landscape – and a wonderful home.

VOEL NANT . TELEGRAPH
Built in 1841 by the
TRUSTEES
of the
LIVERPOOL, DOCKS

8 Foel Nant telegraph station
Sending messages faster than the wind

This building is all about the view. Panoramic views over the Irish Sea, along the north Wales coast. But then this building has always been about the view – strategically located on a hill above the coastline but also with clear views to its west and east. That's because Foel Nant, which was built in 1841, is one of twelve telegraph stations dotted along the north Wales coast between Holyhead Mountain and Liverpool Docks.

On the north Wales coast, overlooking the Irish Sea.

Above left: The telegraph station was perched high on a hill to get the best visibility up and down the coast.

Below left: The makers of this building proudly announce the fact by installing a large stone plaque.

Between them they established a semaphore signalling chain so that advanced warning could be given of merchant shipping sighted off Holyhead, approaching Liverpool Bay. Today, although signalling has long gone, its location plays a big part in its success as a unique family home.

Although originally a place of work, Foel Nant has always been a home. It was home to the telegraph keepers, and the orientation of this little cottage reflects its use as both home and office. It was very important that the part of the building, known as the control room, had clear uninterrupted views up and down the coast, as it was from here that the signals were received and sent. Hence the large curved bay window facing directly north. The trustees of the Liverpool Docks built the chain of stations along the north Wales coast to relay weather and other important information between Anglesey and Liverpool. A message would be received by the first station on Holyhead Mountain from a ship as it passed-by on its way to Liverpool Dock. This message would be passed on, by code, to the next station at 'Cefn Du' near the village of Llanrhyddlad; and then passed to the next station ten miles east, on the north slope of 'Mynydd Eilian' just above Point Lynas, and the next, and so on, through all twelve stations,

83

Old and new – both using a curved shape to obtain the best views.

until it reached its destination in Liverpool Dock. Over time the operators at these stations became so skilled that a shipowner in Liverpool could receive news of his ship off Holyhead (over 90 miles away) in less than a minute. Records describe how, during a trial in 1830 a message went out from Liverpool to Holyhead and a reply was received in just 23 seconds. The system depended on good visibility, and a telescope was used to read off the signals. This sat on a big curved wooden beam within the bay window. But it was an astonishingly quick form of communication. It was claimed that a message could travel faster than the wind.

The appearance of Foel Nant has changed a little since it was last used as a semaphore signalling station. Another curved bay window has been added to one side, and a pitched roof has replaced the flat roof over the office. The two masts that sat on top of the office roof were enormous. I suppose they would have had to be, so they could be seen from quite a

Formerly the office, but now the living room. It was essential to have a panoramic view out along the coast.

distance. Each mast had four signal arms, two on either side. They were operated from the Control Room below. A code was introduced to signify a series of letters and numbers. There were about 40,000 codes in all. Almost anything you wanted to say, there was a code for it.

There would have been two keepers, and it must have been a lonely existence. The first signals would come in soon after dawn, and they would continue all day until sunset. The site is quite remote and they would have been self sufficient, growing their own food in the garden. The underground brick vaulted water tank is still there today, along with the old cast iron pump in the pantry.

Aamon and Moira Jessop bought the house in 1998. Moira had a premonition some years ago that they would land up one day with a house with a bay window looking out over the Irish Sea. When they saw a house fitting that exact description in an estate agent's window they just

High on a hill overlooking the coast with the new wind turbines out at sea.

had to seek it out. Access was difficult, up a remote track, but when they eventually arrived it was exactly what Moira had foreseen. Aamon says "you just get that feeling sometimes that it's the right house for you. And that's what happened. The views you get from here are incomparable. They are priceless. That's the biggest benefit of living here". Aamon also pointed out how windy it gets perched high on a hill next to the sea. It blew part of their garage down on one occasion. So, its not surprising a wind farm has been built directly off the coast.

The house was completely renovated by the previous owners in 1991. The former office has now been converted into a cosy living room with panoramic views over the Irish Sea. The room also retains its original raised platform in the bay window from which the control mechanism once clattered out thousands of codes to guide ships into dock. In the new bay window on the west side of the room a baby grand piano sits quite comfortably providing a centrepiece for parties and sing alongs.

The original house still looks much as it did with its heather blue Penrhyn slates laid in diminishing course over the roof. This exaggerates the perspective of the rows of slate moving further away with each layer. At the ridge there is a charming collection of chimney stacks gathered together in a little group teetering on top of the slates. This grouping reflects the unusual arrangement in the rooms below, where there is a fireplace in the corner of each room backing on to each other.

Inside Moira proudly shows off her special 'Compass Window'. She got help with the design from a local craftsman in the Conwy Valley. She wanted it to be the 'House Compass' – that is, north is on the side of the window pointing in the direction of north. The window is flanked on each side by a row of signal flags, that the keepers would have seen on the ships as they passed by.

One of the most exciting things about renovating an old building is the chance that you might find a small artefact that will link the building to the people who lived there years ago.

One of the most exciting things about renovating an old building is the chance that you might find a small artefact that will link the building to the people who lived there years ago. During the building work in 1991 a small child's shoe was found in the attic. It dates from around 1850 – certainly no earlier as it has machine stitching. Around that time it was a custom that, if a child died, they would place one of their shoes in the attic to keep the spirit close to the family.

The last mechanical telegraph was sent from Foel Nant in 1860. Morse code had been invented and the semaphore masts were replaced with an electric system. The station continued to operate until the early 20th century. As you gaze out to sea, captivated by the row of wind turbines with their arms slowly turning, hypnotising, you can't help but see the similarities with the now lost semaphore masts – the great towers with arms flailing in an effort to do their job. Both play an important role in the industry of their time. As with the semaphore masts, I'm sure these great machines out at sea will have their time and one day be consigned to history, overtaken by another more useful technology.

9

Llewellyn Almshouses
Charity begins at home

Normally, the spectacular can be seen from a long way off. You get some kind of clue to what is around the corner. Maybe you are entering an area that's a bit more 'up-market', and there are other interesting buildings nearby. But nothing prepares you for this small but fanciful building in the back streets of Neath.

Located in the suburbs of Neath.

Tucked away amongst the ordinary terraced houses is this magnificent Gothic gem. The Llewellyn Almshouses were built in 1897 by Lady Llewellyn of Baglan House in memory of her husband Griffith Llewellyn to house the poor and needy.

The Almshouses were built for the single and widowed ladies of the church. There was a great deal of poverty in south Wales at the end of the 19th century and when the servants who had lived on the estate for many years were widowed or could no longer work, they were provided with an alternative to life on the streets. It was a time of great industrial wealth, and this engendered a philanthropic patronage that empowered the rich to do some good for those worse off than themselves. This would have sat comfortably with the resurgence of faith and a period of church building that had not been seen since the Medieval period. In fact, the Llewellyn family were known for their church building, particularly in the Valleys, where they built St Peters Church, commonly known as Rhondda Cathedral.

Almshouses were first recorded in Britain in 10th century York, and there is evidence that the Almhouse is an ancient tradition. The oldest Almshouse in Wales is in Ruthin and was founded in 1590. The word 'Alms' comes from the Greek 'eleemosune' meaning compassion, and there are plenty of examples of the ancient world providing care and hospitality to the sick and poor. Although they can vary in size, style and shape, and can be humble or spectacular, they are most commonly single storey linear

A composition of timber framed gables, red brick and sandstone windows give this building real quality.

groups of cottages, located close to a church. There are 40 trusts in Wales managing nearly 400 Almshouses.

The Llewellyn Almshouses were designed by the diocesan architect George E. Halliday, renowned for his Gothic designs and details, and built by the estate carpenters and masons, utilising the abundant supply of wood from the estate. It is also interesting to note that the surrounding houses are all built from local materials – Pennant Sandstone and Welsh slate. The contrast couldn't be more startling. As a direct show of wealth, the Almshouses were built of the best materials from all around the country – bright red Rhiwabon bricks from north Wales, a golden red carved sandstone surrounding the windows from the south of England, and clay roof tiles, not commonly seen in the area. These materials would certainly make it stand out from the crowd, but it is the elaborate detailing that really makes this building something special.

Above right: The recessed entrance porches make ideal places to sit out and tend plants.
Below right: Curved timber brackets support the roof.

It is a row of eight cottages with a central common room creating a linear frontage with a symmetrical façade, the central gable projecting forward to give a focus to the whole piece. The main façade is virtually unchanged since it was built over a hundred years ago, except for the uncharacteristically plain gable in the roof, where all the others are half-timbered. Later I found an old drawing of the building which showed that this gable was in fact originally half-timbered as well. I thought how complete the building would look if this was fully restored. These half-timbered gables are jettied on brackets and exposed joists, projecting forward and casting heavy shadows in the strong sunlight. Little billet mouldings adorn the timber roof fascias and across the tops of the horizontal members, coming together at the apex with a bossed finial. The brick walls have neat tight joints and are raised on a brick plinth about a metre from the ground. The stone window surrounds are also decorated,

The details in the projecting roof gables and brackets gives this building real depth.

with cinquefoil heads to narrow openings in groups of four, and glazed with simple leaded lights and metal opening windows. This row of Gothic inspired windows is capped with a traditional drip mould designed to throw water away from the window as it runs down the face of the wall – although I'm sure it's more decorative in this instance. The green painted moulded gutters discharge into castellated little hoppers that continue the Gothic theme. Carved stone 'grotesque' heads support the chunky wood brackets, so that every detail is taken care of in this historic *tour de force*. Each entrance is set back under a recessed open porch which it shares with its neighbour. These cosy little entrances face directly south and are perfect for capturing the sunlight. So you can just imagine how useful they are for the residents to sit out on a fine day, encouraging a good community spirit – the odd welcoming plant pot and ornament sitting on the step. It is that human touch that often makes a house into a home – it says someone lives here and cares about this place, and you can see how much the residents love their little building.

Inside, the houses are very small; but arguably adequate for a single person with few needs and possessions – everything is close at hand.

You walk through the front door and straight into the bijou bedsit. A bed, armchair, side table and that's it. The historical half timbered Gothic theme continues. The room is completely panelled with timber from the estate, heavy beams in the ceiling, and an inglenook fireplace that dominates the room. The fireplace has a Tudor arch, and there are a couple of small cupboards built into the panelling on one side. Another traditional feature of this inglenook is the fire window that looks directly out onto the front door. Very useful if you're a single woman living on your own and you want to see who's come calling. On another wall is a built-in dresser with shelves and cup hooks for crockery. A little kitchen and bathroom at the back completes the accommodation. So, although the space is limited everything is there, and it is quite clear that the residents are more than happy with their lot. Originally the bed had its own space where the kitchen is now, as the bathroom was a scullery, and a communal washroom was provided behind the common room. However, some alterations have been made to meet modern standards of living.

A trust was formed to look after the building and its residents when the Almshouses were first built in 1897, and an endowment plan set up by the Llewellyn family to maintain and run the place.

A trust was formed to look after the building and its residents when the Almshouses were first built in 1897, and an endowment plan set up by the Llewellyn family to maintain and run the place. Today the Almshouses continue to be run by a group of trustees, and unusually a member of the original Llewellyn family – Lady Janet Llewellyn, is still a trustee. The Almshouses still provide accommodation according to the original principles. They are provided for women, in order of preference – widowed, single and over 45. If these people could not be found then the criteria would change. Like many social housing schemes, past and present, the residents live to a pronounced set of rules. A copy of the original rule book still exists for the Llewellyn Almshouses and makes fascinating reading, and maybe a small reflection of life at that time. My particular favourite is rule 13: *'Dishonesty, drunkenness, brawling, or immoral or unseemly conduct or behaviour, or any non compliance with these rules*

shall be sufficient cause for removal or expulsion from the benefits of the Almshouses'. What on earth were the ladies of the parish getting up to at the end of the 19th century?

New residents have to make an application to the trustees if they want to occupy one of the houses when they become vacant. Mrs Lotty resides at No.3. She found that after her husband died she couldn't manage the house she was living in as it was too big for her on her own. So an interview was set up with the trustees, and because of her circumstances, and as she belonged to the church, she was offered the place right away. Pat Jones moved out of a three bed house and into these cosy surroundings. Pat remembers the first time she came in and sat down in the armchair just to enjoy the warmth. Her previous house was very cold.

The tradition of Alms Housing still lives on and provides the same benefits as it did many centuries earlier. The Almshouses in Neath are a combination of extraordinary architectural detail, and a worthwhile charitable benefit to the community. It warms the heart to witness such a powerful combination.

The Green Man

The Green Man is the name for a sculpture, drawing or representation of a face surrounded by, or made out of, leaves. Branches or vines may sprout from the nose, mouth or other parts of the face. They were commonly used for decorative architectural ornament, and are frequently found in carvings in churches – appearing on capitols, corbels, choir stalls, bench ends, fonts etc. For the Victorians particularly, they played a major role in church restorations and as decorative motifs on street architecture.

The name Green Man was first used by Lady Raglan in 1939 to describe the head at Llangwm. The earliest examples of the Green Man can be found in the art of Classical Rome. The idea was adopted by Christianity and spread along pilgrimage routes. Examples can be found all over Western Europe and parts of Asia and North Africa.

The Green Man is not a gargoyle – a nightmarish head that projects from the walls of cathedrals and churches – which were placed on buildings to ward off evil. In some cultures, he is interpreted as a symbol of rebirth – the cycle of growth being reborn each Spring.

The central two storey gable, now missing its timber framing above the upper window.

10 Tŷ Gawla, Rudry
Country confusion or a barn storming idea?

For many, living in the countryside has become the ultimate dream, and barn conversions offer the answer to comfortable modern living in traditional surroundings. But, with so many people clambering to the auctions to bid for their rural idyll, it is increasingly difficult to find that beautiful stone barn ripe for conversion. So what is the answer? Build your own barn? Or, take an existing house and convert it into a barn? That is exactly what Ann and Peter Jones did when they were faced with this very same dilemma.

Rudry, near Caerphilly, 10 miles north of Cardiff.

This arrangement provides a contemporary solution to a modern barn.

Ann and Peter were living in a cosy 17th century cottage when they decided to move home in 2002. They came across a house just two miles up the road in a wonderful countryside location with panoramic views over the Bristol Channel. But, whilst the location was perfect, the house was not. So they set about transforming the house into something that would not only suit their purposes, but also sit more comfortably in the landscape. The 1960s and 70s left behind a legacy of buildings that paid very little regard to context, particularly in the rural areas of Wales. We still see far too many buildings that would be more at home in the suburbs or Cardiff than in their native rural setting. They are often hard white rendered boxes, with low pitched roofs, and a token area of stonework. Tŷ Gawla was just such a house. Ann and Peter were very conscious that they had one opportunity to get it right, so they employed one of Wales' leading house designers, Loyn & Co. to come up with an idea that would transform the

97

Above left: Tŷ Gawla nestles into the hillside.
Below left: A second storey was added through the middle of the building.
Right: The balconies on the south side take advantage of the panoramic views.

existing house, and make sure that it sat comfortably in its rural setting.

They felt that a traditional farm building might have sat here in the past, or more likely nestled in the valley sheltering from the harsh climate. Nevertheless, they looked around for clues to inform the design of their new home, and found a fairly modern hay barn nearby. It was clad with vertical timber boards, the gaps between them providing ventilation for the hay so it could remain dry and well aired. It was roofed very simply with corrugated sheeting. It was this simple building that paved the way for the remodelling of Tŷ Gawla. So they set about creating a contemporary barn – a 'Neo-Barn'. The lightweight timber cladding would sit on top of the heavier masonry on the lower floors. This would be particularly useful as they planned on increasing the size of the house by 50% and dealing with the overall mass of the building was an important challenge.

An extra storey has been added to the centre of the building, which has

The main bedroom overlooking the countryside leading down to Cardiff and the Bristol Channel.

become the prominent focal point of the house. As you enter this two storey hall, the whole building opens up into the roof, providing a lofty 'barn-like' feel to the space. The views out from the entrance hall make it feel even more spacious, with the countryside all around you. As project architect Dan Benham explained, "you get sucked into the landscape, and the landscape penetrates the house. The tall glass walls bring the sky into the space, and the views through the dining area are uninterrupted across the balcony because the balustrading is made of totally transparent, frameless glass".

The timber barn theme has been cleverly manipulated into the design. It has been incorporated in a contemporary way on the balustrades of the main stairs, and the balcony off the main living room. But the most ingenious use of the vertical wooden boarding is in the external wall cladding. A modern house these days craves as much daylight as possible,

The kitchen and living room provide views down to Cardiff and the coast.

and opening up views over the surrounding landscape is particularly desirable in such a beautiful setting. But large areas of glass do not work well with the barn concept. So many of the windows have been disguised behind timber cladding, using larger gaps between boards to allow the light in and views out. This particular detail has been carried off with great skill. It creates interest as your eye passes over the external walls, allowing you to unravel the different layers of materials on this unique building. The roof is made of zinc sheeting, which continues the barn theme.

Even the ridge is large and bulky, something you're more likely to find on an industrial building rather than a house. It is this attention to detail and the use of materials that hold the concept together well. I was particularly taken by the use of the local Pennant stone for some of the walls. Normally you would use the natural or dressed face on the outside giving an uneven rustic appearance – very natural. But the stone has been turned around so that the clean cut side faces out and forms the main face of the wall. This provides a modern interpretation of the traditional stone wall, and it works, because it is still the local natural material, but used in

This intriguing collection of wood, stone and glass provides an artistic arrangement in the landscape.

a contemporary way. Instead of introducing off-the-shelf vents in the wall, they have been created out of long slithers of the same stone so there is little interruption to the material.

Wherever you go in the building there is a view to be seen. The house has been orientated so that the main living room, dining area, and kitchen with breakfast room, all face the views south. The spaces are very open so you get glimpses of views through adjacent rooms. This helps bring light deeper into the building and gives the impression of even more space.

The master bedroom is the only room on the upper floor that faces south and is also very exposed. But the views are breathtaking. I suppose you would get used to undressing in front of the capital city at night. Maybe curtains would be a good idea!

Ann was very insistent that she had a room where they could retreat to, a more cosy intimate space. The furniture in the snug is very traditional and has been brought from their previous 17th century home. It's a nice contrast to the openness of the rest of the house, and it works well. The view out of the full height window is beautifully framed with a small alpine garden, big old trees along a wooden fence and distant fields. This has become a very important area for Ann and Peter.

Although the house has been remodelled out of all recognition, there are areas of the original house that still survive. The living room is still housed in the old end of the house. It has been decorated with a more contemporary colour scheme, as have the wooden trusses to the open roof. It is easy to forget, in this neo-barn conversion, that it is not a barn. If you walked into a modern barn conversion you would expect to see some of the traditional features retained and shown off. The irony is that the traditional 'king post' trusses over the living room, with their heavy iron straps, are modern and actually came from the 1970s house. So who's copying who?

Tŷ Gawla is a product of a modern rural concept – taking the charm of something essentially agricultural, and making it into a dwelling.

Left: The main hall with its timber stairs and bridge.
Above: A new composition for the Welsh countryside.

Tŷ Gawla is a product of a modern rural concept – taking the charm of something essentially agricultural, and making it into a dwelling. I wonder what our forefathers would have thought about us wanting to live in 'the cowshed'. The barn conversion is a successful modern idea that is fast running out of energy, and so the idea will need to be re-invented.
The original Tŷ Gawla has been completely transformed, and even if you look carefully you'll hardly recognise any traces of the earlier house. This is an extraordinary idea. Maybe it is a reflection of our current obsession with barn conversions and living in the countryside.

But has it worked? When the cedar boarding weathers to a muted grey colour and blends with the stone walls and the roof, the building will gently melt back into the countryside. So, although it is bigger than the original house, it will probably fit into the landscape far better. Trying to bring the 'big barn' idea to a dwelling is a brave and admirable concept and it is refreshing to see such thought going into design, particularly in the Welsh countryside. If you ignore the fact that the main two storey barn at Tŷ Gawla is rather engulfed by the surrounding attached buildings in a way you would not see on any agricultural complex, then you would have to say it has brought a new form of rural architecture to the Welsh countryside, and for that it should be applauded.

11 Sunningdale, Tŷ Draw Road
Sweetness and light in the suburbs

Wherever you go in Cardiff you are likely to see row upon row of Edwardian terraced houses. They represent the distinctive character of the capital city, at a time when Cardiff was put on the map by a boom period of industry and house building. To see the real splendour of Edwardian housing I visited Tŷ Draw Road in Cardiff where there is a rich variety of detached, semi-detached, and terraced houses in one of the most sought after addresses in the City.

Situated facing the southern section of Roath Park in Cardiff.

Sunningdale lies at one end of Tŷ Draw Road and faces onto the southern section of Roath Park. Writer Mike Smith and his partner Robin had restored two Victorian properties before buying Sunningdale, so they had some experience with old properties. But this was a far larger house with its 5 bedrooms and 2 bathrooms, and took almost two years to complete. The house was totally unmodernised, which meant on the one hand it retained a lot of original features, but on the other it was in an unliveable condition. There was a huge amount of work to be done.

So, for the first year they employed a builder to undertake all the major jobs. Mike recalls how all the hall walls were covered with Lincrusta – a patented heavily embossed kind of wallpaper, made of chalk and linseed oil. It was dark brown and it took many weeks removing it – it had to be chipped off piece by piece with chisels. Decorating and furnishing a period property can be difficult, but Mike and Robin have carried this off with great style, mixing good period pieces with contemporary décor, and the occasional quirky object.

Sunningdale as seen from Roath Park.

Sunningdale is semi-detached and displays typical Edwardian features such as tile hanging, large windows, and a balcony.

These grand Edwardian houses were built to standards set down by the richest man in the world at the end of the 19th century – the Third Marquis of Bute. But his architectural influence went beyond the grandeur of what he created at Cardiff Castle. These, and many other houses in Cardiff, were also shaped by his vision. His life long interest in architecture grew out of his interest in the Medieval. He was passionate about old castles, monasteries and churches, and at Cardiff Castle when he was just 18 he asked his architect, William Burgess to re-design it. The land upon which Sunningdale sits was part of the Bute Estate, but it was very marshy and

any part thereof cause a covenant to the like effect as
that if the rent hereby reserved or any part thereof shall
ance of any of the covenants and agreements herein cor
me of the whole wholly to re-enter and the same to have
h hereby covenant with the said Lessee   that the said I
erformed shall and may peaceably possess and enjoy t
of the said parties to these presents have hereunto set the

The lease signed by Lord Bute's own solicitor, W Thomas Lewis.

boggy, and it would be very expensive to drain the land in order to build houses upon it. So the Bute authorities gave it to the local council upon which they built a public park. The council spent their own money draining the site and making the park, saving the Estate a considerable expense, and also making the land around the park fit for building houses upon. They built some of the best houses in Cardiff. I met up with Matthew Williams, curator of Cardiff Castle and an expert on the Bute Family, to look over the house. I was curious to learn what kind of person this house might have been built for. The records show that Sunningdale was lived in by a maiden lady in the first few years, and was then sold to a solicitor, who retained it for the next 20 years. Most of the houses around this area were lived in by professional men. Matthew and I were able to study the original lease for Sunningdale, a large single piece of parchment with a red wax seal at the bottom. The 99 year lease was granted by the Bute Estate to a local builder. The street with various plots are drawn out on the parchment with a building shown on Sunningdale's plot. It clearly indicates that the land was being sold with a building already designed for it. As Matthew said, 'It's all about control'. The Bute Estate controlled everything that was to be built on their land, including the design of the houses. By the look

of the seal on the Lease, they also took a personal interest too. This lease was signed by W Thomas Lewis, Bute's own solicitor, and some Leases were signed by the Marquis himself.

To bring a cohesive look to the properties on Bute land, the Estate employed its own architect, Edward Corbett. He was responsible not only for the grand houses such as Sunningdale, but also the more modest terraced houses, like those at Hirwaun Street. They may be smaller but they derive their simple and less expensive details from the more affluent houses. For example, the main room fireplace may be identical to one in the servant's bedroom at Sunningdale. After all, the same class of person would be living there.

Sunningdale has got all the characteristics you would expect to find in an Edwardian Villa.

Taking a closer look at Sunningdale we can see that it has got all the characteristics you would expect to find in an Edwardian Villa. The use of stone for window surrounds and lintols, terracotta tile hanging in the gable, and rich red clay bricks. Although Matthew pointed out that this is probably a lot plainer than houses built ten years earlier as there is no carving on the stonework, and it is in a Arts & Crafts style. A deeply set back porch was another feature of this period, creating a cosy welcome to the visitor. Also noticeable are the large windows and the complete absence of glazing bars. As glass technology improved, panes of glass became larger, until in the early 1900s many windows had no glazing bars at all, and where more appropriate than overlooking the park. This is in complete contrast to a typical Georgian window with its many small panes of glass. It was also common to embellish some of these plain windows with areas of leaded lights and glass. Lead lights are used on a first floor window with Art Nouveau decoration sweeping across the panes of coloured glass.
It is done in a very subtle and delicate way, and this subtlety can been seen throughout the house. The house also takes its influence from the Queen Anne Movement, with their concern for 'Sweetness & Light', characterised in the upper middle class areas of Cardiff with balconies, balconettes, and railings. It was born out of their concern for fresh air, light and space – a development and contrast to the Victorian fashion of dark rooms and heavy cluttered decoration.

Inside there is a grand entrance hall just as you would expect to find it.

A spacious landing on two levels, looking towards the front of the house from the servants quarters.

A grand entrance with decorative coving, a wide timber stairs and encaustic floor tiles.

It has a tiled floor, an arch separating the outer hall from the inner hall that contains the large wooden staircase. There is a dentilled and bracketed cove to the ceiling more reminiscent of Victorian than Edwardian. Although the design of the house was all done for the builder, he was allowed to add his own fixtures and fittings, such as coving, doors, fireplaces etc. These were selected from a pattern book and, not having the eye or the taste of the architect, the builder often chose out of date or contradicting styles.

Sunningdale shows very clearly in its architecture the different class structure in the house. The front of the house is where the owners lived, characterised by the taller ceilings, a variety of grand marble fireplaces in living rooms and bedrooms, and the wider architraves around doors, and taller skirtings. The servants lived at the rear of the house where the features are more subdued – narrower architraves, and lower ceilings. The fireplaces are smaller and made of cast iron. All the features throughout the house are an expression of who lived where, and what status they held. Whilst Cardiff has an abundance of Edwardian houses there are none better than those in Tŷ Draw Road, and probably few display as many original features as Sunningdale. These houses also demonstrate

...in bedroom
...ce made up of
...c styling, with
...al pilasters, Art
...u brass hood,
...torian tiling.

Left: Art Nouveau glass door leading to the balcony.
Above left: Ornate brass finger plates and door knobs to all the main rooms.
Above right: The servants fireplaces were much smaller, but still delicately designed.

that the Edwardians had just about reached the end of a long period of development in house design. It had started with the Georgian terrace and then developed through to the Victorian period and finally, at the beginning of the 20th century, the Edwardian house. The houses are light and sociable, and have an enduring quality about them, as they are still very relevant to the way we live today. The same houses are expressed as grand villas or, with a similar floor plan, as a small terraced house.

Sadly, so many of these simple terraces have been stripped of their Edwardian character, owners preferring to modernise their home by carrying out 'improvements' such as replacing slate with concrete tiles, and perfectly good sliding sash windows with PVC. But there are those who take a more sympathetic view and see the extra benefits that these houses can offer, like Mike and Robin have done.

12 Treowen
A noble mansion of pleasing decay

Visiting this house is like stepping back into the 17th century where very little has changed for hundreds of years. Treowen is one of those little gems that you didn't know existed, and yet it is only four miles outside Monmouth, and set in a beautiful rolling landscape, surrounded by acres of woodland and views over the Black Mountains and Brecon Beacons. Furthermore, you can have it all to yourself; the whole house, as it can be rented out for parties, weddings or whatever you like.

Four miles outside Monmouth with views over the Black Mountains and Brecon Beacons.

A sublime landscape as seen through the front porch at Treowen.

Treowen's special historic character and rarity has been recognised by being listed as a Grade One property, and is unusual for the way it has been preserved and looked after. So many of our ancient historic houses have been over restored into pristine condition, or as a representation of what the owner thinks history looks like. The present owners of this building have laid their hands very gently on this fine and noble building, careful not to replace old features just because they look decayed and worn. This is a classic example of 'pleasing decay'.

Imagine being whisked off to the Welsh countryside to live in a big old rambling house as a child. That is what happened to Dick and John Wheelock at the ages of six and eight years old. Their grandfather was a very successful stockbroker who made himself a fortune and in 1954 decided he should set his youngest son up in a style he wished him to become accustomed to. He bought him Treowen for the sum of £25,000. Dick and John remember the adventures they had climbing what seemed like every tree on the 150 acres of woodland, discovering hiding holes in

Left: The magnificent three story porch with its columns and armorial features.
Above: The main front of Treowen. It was originally three storey like the rear section, before it was reduced in height.

the house, and digging in the garden to look for secret tunnels. But looking after such a big old house was an expensive business, and their father decided the best thing to do was to give it to his two sons.

They didn't really want it, as they both had well paid jobs and didn't want to pour their salaries into repairing the house. But then John lost his job as an accountant, and thought about making the house pay for itself. After all, he had just spent the last seven years telling other people how to run their businesses – "why don't I put it into practice myself", and holiday letting seemed to be the right thing. "People like coming here, even in winter".

Treowen was built in 1627 and has a 'double pile' plan – in other words it is like have two buildings pushed together, one behind the other. It was built by William Jones after inheriting a fortune from his uncle. He decided to rebuild the previous house to create something more modern. It was a very large house by local standards but shortly afterwards they thought it looked a bit austere so they added a beautiful tall entrance porch to the front, displaying the Jones coat of arms. The most notable alteration to Treowen is the loss of the top story to the front face of the house, which when originally built would have been the same height as the back. You can imagine how plain the house must have looked – a big lump of a building!

The fine wooden screen at the entrance to the Great Hall was only reinstated in 2001.

The porch and the reduced height certainly make for a more pleasing composition, particularly with the columns and decorative strapwork adorning the porch. However, I'm sure it would have been more successful if they had managed to line things up a bit better – the side walls of the porch seem to crash into the windows, and the string courses on the porch and main building do not line through. Nevertheless, it is a magnificent feature to greet any visitor.

On entering the building it still has a wonderful medieval feel to it. On the left of the passage is where, traditionally, the kitchens were, whilst on the right, behind a magnificent decorated oak screen is the Banquetting Hall. This method of separation between the noise and mayhem of the kitchens, and the Lord and his guests, remained part of Country House design for many centuries. Hence it was known as a 'screens passage'. The screen was removed from Treowen in 1898 because the tenant farmer was using the Hall to store grain that was causing the bottom of the screen to rot. It was restored to it original position by Dick and John in 2001. Over the two doors are the initials of Williams Jones and the date 1627.

As you continue through the house you come across Treown's most notable feature. The Grand Stairs. This is what the house is all about

Below: The earliest open well staircase in the country, and Treowen's most notable feature.

– massive strength and simplicity. It is reputed to be the earliest open well staircase in the country. It is quite a sight standing at the bottom looking up through the middle of the stairs, rising up four storeys through the height of the building. The short flights are five feet wide, the oak balusters beautifully turned, the newel posts are topped with vase finials, and they all have that hand made imperfection about them. This epitomises the Jacobean character of the house. Some of the newels are chipped and scarred from years of use.

Situated on the first floor is the Great Chamber, a room originally occupied by the ladies of the house, directly above the Banqueting Hall. Half of the deeply patterned plaster ceiling is missing, and this typifies the approach that the present owners have taken to keeping the house. Maybe it's down to the cost of putting the ceiling back, or maybe it follows

Left: The Hall screen is very finely carved and in excellent condition considering it lay rotting in a barn for many years. Above: This oak door is centuries old and exudes character. It has not been over restored – the rust and grain of the timber look beautiful.

a 'simply repair' philosophy, but the remains of the ceiling reflect its journey through history, and the alterations and lack of investment it has undergone through the centuries. It does look a little sad and forlorn, and yet somehow defiantly proud as well. The walls were probably originally covered with carved wooden panelling, and the room full of oak furniture.

Dick and John keep chipping away at this big old beast, continually repairing and restoring, but in a very simplistic way. When I visited Treowen Dick was busy making carpentry repairs, and on that scale it seems likely he will be there for the rest of his life, working at his own pace. But their obvious love and enthusiasm for the house drives them on. This is evident when you hear them telling stories about the house. John showed me a 'Priest Hole' they discovered under the first floor landing. The Joneses were a Catholic family and lived in the troubled times of the Civil War and the Restoration. There were plenty of stories of them celebrating Mass when it was forbidden by law to do so. Hiding holes such as this one were probably for hiding the chalice and vestments rather than a priest. When they cleared out all the debris they found a small picture of Mary Magdalene amid the several inches of dust. More recent stories include the one where Queen Victoria was being chased up the Grand

Treowen sitting proudly
in its landscape.

Stairs by aliens – well it was used as a set for Doctor Who a few months earlier.

Because many of the original embellishments of the house are missing, the place does feel more austere than it perhaps once did. However, as you explore the maze of rooms you can still appreciate the history hidden in the walls of this old pile; every room still has its original crumbling stone mullioned windows with leaded glass; the servants' spiral stairs are made up of quartered oak steps; a door frame has a curved chunk taken out of it, believed to be where barrels were hoisted through the opening and in through a nearby window; and there are many big old stone fireplaces dotted around the place.

Although the house is available to the public for hire, the Wheeler family still use the house themselves for special occasions, and recently had a family Christmas dinner for 38 people, with venison that was raised on their land. John says he is proud of what he has achieved, and recalls what his father said when he tried to persuade him to sell Treowen – "my father bought it for me, and now I'm giving it to you". John thinks his father would approve of what they've made of Treowen today. (www.treowen.co.uk)

Below: A stone mullioned window partly decayed but still in working order.

Pleasing Decay

Celebrated artist John Piper wrote about Pleasing Decay in an article for the Architectural Review in September 1947. He argued that old buildings are often ruthlessly restored in such a way that the effects of age are stripped away in favour of a new clean appearance, and in so doing the building loses its venerability. Buildings often take on a patina with age and this should be respected as the natural aging process of the building.

Piper claims 'the natural weathering of a surface of a building is beautiful, and its loss disastrous'. An old wall is generally covered with lime plaster and over time this takes on an uneven appearance and the light reflects off its surface highlighting every bump and crack. Sadly this plaster is often replaced with a modern hard flat plaster that drains all the life and character out of the wall. Similarly ancient stones are often needlessly replaced simply because they look weathered. The temptation to 'iron out the creases' in old buildings should be resisted. Using a light hand when making repairs will preserve the very character that attracted you to the building in the first place.

13 The Hall, Abbey Cwm Hir
Restoring Victorian splendour

Finding that beautiful run down old house in the country and spending your time carefully restoring it to its former glory is something many of us will have dreamed about.
But I imagine that dream did not include a 52 room mansion. That is exactly what a couple have spent the past eight years doing, and they have re-created one of Wales' finest Victorian country houses. For Paul and Victoria Humpherston this house has been one big labour of love.

Ten miles north of Llandrindod Wells.

The village of Abbey Cwm Hir takes its name from the Cistercian monastic ruins that were built in 1143. Cwm Hir means *long valley* after the long curving vale that cuts through this part of the Radnorshire hills. The Hall was built by Francis Aspinall Philips in around 1867 and is nicely paired with the nearby parish church, both designed by the same architect. It is designed in the high Victorian Gothic Revival style, with steeply pitched gables and elaborately decorated fascias, and finials. The Victorians were great antiquarians and revelled in recreating historical styles, particularly Gothic. Many of these details can be found on more modest Victorian terraced houses, but this is the high end of Victorian style where no expense was spared. The Hall is built from top quality Ashlar stonework with intricately carved details around windows and beautifully carved stone brackets supporting the timber roof fascias. The entrance porch is typically Victorian with its Gothic arch of alternating red and cream coloured stones, heraldic motifs, and red granite columns. This is what the Victorians do best, and The Hall is an excellent example.

Designed in the high Victorian Gothic Revival style, with steeply pitched gables and elaborately decorated fascias and finials.

By the late 1990s the best days of The Hall at Abbey Cwm Hir had gone and it was in deep need of tender loving care. When Paul and Victoria found Abbey Cwm Hir they instantly fell in love with the place. So they paid £495,000 for what was to become a 52 room restoration project. They say they had no doubts, and have always wanted to live in Wales, but Paul does remember quivering a bit at the thought of the amount of work that was needed. This would have been a serious project for a commercial developer, but for a private couple hoping to make it their home, the sheer effort required beggars belief. I don't think I have ever come across a project of this scale, undertaken privately. The work involved re-roofing, re-wiring and renewing all the drainage. Inside the decoration varied from complete repainting to taking up floorboards and replacing ceilings. Sometimes this involved lots of research so that they could be redesigned and restored to how they were originally. Paul and Victoria believe very strongly in bringing things back to the way they were intended.

Below: A painted scene of children visiting The Hall on New Year's Eve in 1899 by Robert Parkin.

From the outside, The Hall looks like a beautifully restored country house. But when you walk through the stone porch and into the hall you start to realise that there's something extraordinary about this house. The interiors of The Hall are extremely lavish, and a feast of architectural detail. Above the finely carved wooden staircase is a lantern covered with decorated plasterwork. It would be at home in one of William Burgess' creations or adorning the entrance of a Town Hall.

To the left of the entrance hall is the Drawing Room, which at one time was the Ballroom, and clearly the principal room of the house. Robert Parkin, a local artist, was commissioned to undertake ten major scenes depicting the village of Abbey Cwm Hir at various moments in history. These includes – 13th century Knights being blessed by the Abbot of the monastery; Children visiting The Hall on New Years' Eve in 1899; the harvest of 1912; and my favourite, a scene of The Hall at dusk with the windows of the Ballroom lit up, conveying the feeling of a house being used as a home. These paintings give The Hall a sense of place, and although The Hall is only a hundred years old it has been the centre of village life for all these years and is now the keeper of village history. The wallpaper

Left: The stone entrance porch at The Hall, dated 1869.

Above: The knights of the round table are painted on the walls surrounding the Billiard Room.

and wooden shutters of the Ballroom have been embellished by Victoria's William Morris inspired paint effects, and the decorative ceiling cove has been re-gilded, taking hours of painstaking work, as well as great skill.

As I left the Drawing Room and crossed the hallway, beyond the library, I didn't think that things could get any more extraordinary. But they did. The Billiard Room is a *tour de force*. A rectangular room with a bay window at one end. The ceiling is vaulted and crowned with a large lantern light. At the centre of the room is a magnificent billiard table made by Orme & Sons, Billiard Table Builders of London, Manchester & Glasgow, and appointed by HRH Prince of Wales. The table has a top that is inlaid with lines of fleurs-de-lys, and large turned wooden candle sticks on each corner. Two lighting canopies also adorned with the fleurs-de-lys hang over the table. The table has all its fittings and score boards, and everything is just as it was when it was installed in 1894. It is as if they had just put down their cues and left the room for a break. Paul tells of a local legend that Abbey Cwm Hir is Camelot and in reverence of this story he has painted the names of the Knights of the Round Table around the walls of the room, in old English script. It is not just the room and the original fittings that give

Left: Making an entrance at The Hall.
Above: A real eclectic mix that is in complete contrast to the Victorian splendour in the rest of house.

this place such an authentic atmosphere. The Victorians loved to collect and fill every available space with ornaments and curios, and this is where the house is so successful. It is the added value that Paul and Victoria have brought to this house – stuffed animal heads on the wall, elaborately carved furnishings, there is even a stuffed cheetah that used to belong to the daughter of Marlene Dietrich. It is this kind of attention to detail that makes the house what it is today.

They have collected so much of their furniture and bits-and-pieces along the way – mainly from around mid Wales. But the collections are not just confined to Victoriana. At the back of the house, where the outbuildings were slightly detached, Paul and Victoria have made their 'chill out' space, a special place for parties. It is here where there are even more surprises. There are more than 130 enamelled signs covering the brick walls, bicycles and lanterns suspended off the walls and ceilings, a full size red telephone box, and the very last petrol pump from Llandrindod Wells. There is a bar at one end, and a huge television. Big sofas, and pub tables and stools. This is a real eclectic mix that is a complete contrast to the Victorian theme, but nevertheless still continues the idea of filling every available space. There was so much to look at, I was almost relieved to take a walk

A typical bedroom
at The Hall.

outside and take in the natural beauty of the countryside, and their lovely
walled garden.

All this furniture must take an age to keep clean. Victoria agrees.
She recalls how her son came to stay and volunteered to vacuum the
carpets. He thought it might take a few hours – in the end it took him
three days non-stop. Paul says that if you think of all the people who have
lived here and how important the house is to the village, they are the least
distinguished people to have owned the house. Victoria certainly feels she
is one of a dying breed – a home maker. "That's what I do" she says.
The main difference is that they have had to work for their wealth, unlike
their predecessors who inherited theirs.

Below: The ceiling over the main stairs would be at home in a William Burgess interior.

Having spent the eight years restoring The Hall, and coming to the end of such an epic journey, what about the future? Was there a purpose in this venture? Paul wants to ensure that the standards they have set are maintained, and wants The Hall to remain splendid. The Hall could become an exclusive guest house for the wealthy, or a venue for business meetings. In such private and beautiful surroundings, maybe a summit meeting. Since I visited, the Humpherstons have played host to Bollywood, The Hall being used as a film set. Whatever comes to Abbey Cwm Hir, one thing is certain for Paul and Victoria, The Hall at Abbey Cwm Hir will always remain their home. (www.abbeycwmhir.com)

14 Plas Llanmihangel
A most complete manor house

It never ceases to amaze me how many wonderful places there are to stay in Wales, in such beautiful surroundings, and this building is right up there with the best. You can stay the night in this amazing Tudor manor house and be provided with not only a warm and comfortable welcome and fine home-made cooking, but also a truly historic experience.

A couple of miles south of Cowbridge, in the Vale of Glamorgan.

The entrance court is no longer surrounded by a twelve foot high wall, and has an unusual turret in one corner.

Set in a small hamlet among the rolling farmland of the Vale of Glamorgan is one of the finest and most complete examples of an early Gentry House. But it is the more recent years that also play such a big part in Plas Llanmihangel's history, thanks to the dedication of two extraordinary people. David and Sue Beer have devoted their lives to restoring a building that was on the verge of dereliction and have now created one of the most wonderful Bed & Breakfast places anywhere in the country... although the work still goes on, as I found out when I visited them on a very warm summer's day.

The village of Plas Llanmihangel is made up of an ancient parish church, a fine group of farm buildings, now sadly converted into a modern dwelling, and the magnificent manor house. The house itself is listed as a Grade One and is a sprawling ensemble of stone gables, turrets, dormer windows and chimneys. The layout is quite confusing really, as it doesn't conform to what you might expect a manor house to look like. Although it was first built in the 14th century, only the cellars remain from that period, as the house was largely rebuilt in the 16th century giving it the Tudor and Elizabethan appearance we see today. It is quite rare to find a house of this period that isn't decayed or abandoned, and its original appearance so intact. Its main features include a remarkable panelled hall with a moulded plaster ceiling, stone vaulted cellars, mural stairs (that is, stairs

Plas Llanmihangel comprises the manor house, barn, and a church, and is set in a wooded landscape.

built within the thickness of a wall) and lots of masonry detail, such as the dressed-stone doorways. It reminded me so much of Sker House near Porthcawl, a building I spent many years restoring, but Plas Llanmihangel is far less formal, and has a more lived-in feel. Like Sker House, it maintains the traditions of the medieval first floor Hall, a tradition that seems to have hung on in Wales for many years into the Elizabethan era.

Building a house during this period you would be concerned about defence, ensuring that you could protect yourself if you came under attack. Plas Llanmihangel was no different – the windows on the ground floor would not have existed; or if they did, would have been very small, and the entrance may have been on the first floor making it difficult to breach. For the same reason, living in a first floor Hall goes back to the need to defend yourself, as can be seen in the Norman motte and bailey castles, where the main living accommodation was built high up on a mound or motte. What we can't see now at Plas Llanmihangel are the 12 feet high stone walls that surrounded the south side of the building with a defensible gatehouse in its south west corner.

David and Sue came across the house in the 1980s when visiting a cousin they hadn't seen for 30 years. Sue hadn't been to south Wales before

Above: The main front façade with its shortened wing on the right, is dominated by a collection of stone mullioned windows, and turrets. Below: Stone gargoyle projecting from corner turret.

and thought it was just full of chimneys. She was shocked to see how beautiful it was. Even though it had been continually occupied throughout much of its history, Plas Llanmihangel was looking rather sad and forlorn. With an asking price of just £130,000 there were very few takers, such was the condition of the building and the task ahead for anyone foolish enough to take it on. I think the challenge would have appealed to David and Sue – the architect and the archivist; the architecture and the history. It is a dynamic combination with the ability to research methodically and accurately, and then design and physically restore the details of the past. Nevertheless it's a painstaking process.

The Hall is the centrepiece of the building, and undoubtedly always has been. It is beautifully panelled with oak moulded panels of the 17th century, and the ceiling is distinguished as having the finest Elizabethan decorative plasterwork in Glamorgan with a typical repeating geometric pattern. It has an extraordinary stone fireplace decorated with armorial shields, most of which represent the Thomas family. However, by strange coincidence one of the shields belongs to the De La Bere family, the name of the current owners. The records show that in about 1539 the Hall had been used as a court room, where the Lord of the Manor would have

The Hall is the centrepiece of the house with its panelled walls and the finest Elizabethan decorative plaster ceiling in Glamorgan.

Above: The end panel over the fireplace displays the shield of the De La Bere family, whilst a portrait of Catherine Braganza hangs on the end wall.

sat in judgement on matters of petty crime, such as stealing chickens, drunkenness and brawling etc. and this explains why Henry VIII's coat of arms is displayed at one end of the Hall. One of the other discoveries made by Sue was the identity of a rather regal looking lady in a painting hanging on the wall of The Hall. Noticing she was wearing ermine, normally reserved for royalty, she managed to identify her as Catherine Braganza (1638-1705) queen to King Charles II. I am always concerned about paintings and fittings belonging to a particular house or building. They are often as much about the history of the house as the ceilings or fireplaces, and they really bring the history of a place to life. Sue assured me that she felt the same and to ensure that the painting is never separated from Plas Llanmihangel it is now included in the deeds for the house.

All this research and careful restoration has given David and Sue an unprecedented knowledge of their home, and as you walk through each room the layers of history unfold, as do the storeys of the past owners of this fine house. Opening the heavy oak doors to the Parlour you immediately notice that the style of wooden panelling changes. It's like opening the door to another period in history. The panelling is now much heavier, with more brightly coloured bolection mouldings and raised

The Parlour is an
18th century panelled
room and altogether
quite different to the
rest of the house.

panels, an altogether more gentrified room of the early 18th century.
This room was created by Sir Humphrey Edwin, a man of great importance
in London. Sir Humphrey was a wiley gentleman who always fancied his
own country estate. The Thomas family who owned Plas Llanmihangel at
the time, had never financially recovered from the Civil War. Sir Humphrey
gradually bought up all their debts until, when he bought the last one,
he bankrupted the Thomas family and got, not just the house, but the
whole estate for a fraction of its value.

I have always been intrigued by the way man leaves his mark on
buildings, whether it's during their construction, or by simply using the
building throughout the centuries. One of the more extraordinary ways
this manifests itself at Plas Llanmihangel is on a stone doorway outside
the kitchen. On one side of the stone frame there are deep scars cut into
the surface. Sue explained how this particular door frame has been used
for centuries as a knife sharpener, and how she continues that tradition
by sharpening her own knives there. On the ground floor the door frames
have different marks. Sue showed me a mark resembling a 12 in Roman
numerals (XII), one on each side of the door cut into the stone frame.
Sue believed that, as the frame is made up of several pieces of stone,

Below left: Sunlight streams in through a Hall window.
Below right: The worn stone steps and large oak handrails convey the age and character of the place.

they were assembly marks indicating where each piece of stone should be positioned. This is normally the case in timber frame construction and is commonly found in roofs, as they were made on the ground in various lengths of timber, taken apart to make it easier to haul up to roof level, and then re-assembled. The marks help to identify the many pieces and how they go together. I felt Sue's doors displayed the less commonly found 'masons marks', possibly identifying the actual mason himself – a bit like a signature. This was then hidden by the overlapping wall plaster.

But the most intriguing mystery was on the floor of one of the bedrooms – cross swords cut into very old and worn flagstones. Sue explained that the cross swords represented the Cavaliers, and that the Thomas family were staunch Royalists. Could this be a 'hoard hole'? A place for hiding treasure? Unfortunately the Victorians built an internal dividing wall right over the flagstone, and therefore it cannot be lifted without breaking it. Sue believes that, as the Thomas' left Plas Llanmihangel penniless, they are unlikely to have left anything of value behind. In any case, some mysteries are best left that way.

The layout of the house is confusing, but creates an interesting collection of gables, turrets and roofs.

Plas Llanmihangel is one of those remarkable places that tells us so much about history, both architecturally and socially. For two decades David and Sue Beer have been completely absorbed by this most captivating of houses, and their passion for Plas Llanmihangel shows no sign of diminishing. They are quite philosophical about the whole project. "People ask if this is a five year project? A ten year project...? The minute you start thinking about finishing, it becomes a burden. We know we won't finish it. We just do the best we can." (Phone 01446 774610)

Marks on buildings

If you look very carefully you can often find curious markings on old buildings that do not form conventional architectural decoration. They can often be tucked away out of sight if they were not meant to be seen. The most common are carpenters' marks, which formed part of the assembly process of most timber framed buildings and roofs. The marks usually form a numerical sequence that helped the builder know which timbers to join together. However, the marks found on stonework were quite different, and were carved into the surface of the stone to denote the work of each mason. This was monogrammatic and enabled the mason to get paid for his work. It also identified the person to blame if the work was badly done.

These marks should not be confused with ritual marks. These symbols can be found scratched into timber beams, over fireplaces for example, and also on plaster work, the most common of which is a daisy wheel, and can be found in many old churches. They are thought to have protected against ill-fortune or be a symbol of good luck. Another common mark to be found on old buildings is graffiti. We tend to think that graffiti is a modern practice, but it has been daubed and scratched onto buildings for many centuries.

15 Cefn Mably
A Phoenix from the ashes

This particular property is very close to my heart. In fact, I know every inch of the building, as I was responsible for planning its restoration. This was the 45th house I had visited on my journey around Wales looking at a huge variety of houses, so it was very pleasing for me to show Jane and the crew around this magnificent old building – a building that was described in 1891 as *'one of the finest and most historic country seats in Wales'* (Cardiff Times 1891).

Just north of the M4 motorway, near Cardiff Gate.

Cefn Mably can be seen just north of the M4 motorway, near Cardiff Gate. A fire had devastated the building in 1994 shortly after it was purchased by a developer, leaving it in a completely ruinous state. It was roofless, floorless, and in a perilous condition. The very idea of rescuing what was left of the building was being seriously questioned. Was it viable? And bearing in mind the amount of original historic fabric that had been lost, was it worth it? But the Local Authority were determined that they should not give up on this old building just yet, and along with Cadw they insisted that a scheme was prepared to rescue the building. It was clear that the costs of restoration and conversion would be in excess of what the property was going to be worth, and some other financial incentive was required. The Local Authority agreed to allow the developer to build additional houses in the grounds, thereby gaining enough profit from the sale of the new houses to make the whole project worthwhile.

The restored Cefn Mably with the Chapel in the foreground and the 18th century wing at the far end.

The fire in 1994 exposed the many layers of history in the building. Notice the modern steel roof trusses.

The property eventually changed hands and it was Meadgate Homes of Cardiff who employed my company to prepare designs for its restoration and conversion into 13 luxury apartments.

It was a strange moment for me when I first visited the burnt out ruin. I was trying hard to remember the parts of the building I used to visit as a ten year old boy. My father and I used to accompany the local priest to the Chapel in Cefn Mably once a month to say Mass. I was an altar boy in a nearby Catholic church and I was often invited to help with the service. In later years as youths, my friends and I would camp out by the river just below the house. How sad the building looked now. There was rubbish piled high around the back of the building, a group of youths were drinking and taking drugs, and a man walked straight passed me coming out of the building with a big piece of dressed stone mounted on his shoulder. I didn't dare suggest he was stealing important historic artefacts from a listed building. So I just gave him a nod, and went on my way.

The history of Cefn Mably spans more than 900 years. The first house was built around 1150 on the ridge (*Cefn*) by Mable (*Mably*) daughter of Robert Fitzhamon, the Norman conqueror of Cardiff and Newport. By the 15th century the house had passed into the ownership of the renowned

This 1908 photograph from Country Life magazine, enabled the porch to be recreated accurately.

Kemeys family. During the Civil War the house was fortified and defended against parliament. Sir Nicholas Kemeys, one of the great characters of Cefn Mably, was knighted for saving the life of King Charles I at the Battle of Naseby in 1645, and died leading a defence of Chepstow Castle in 1648. However, he is remembered in a number of 17th century poems, one of which recalls a challenge set down by a Cornish wrestler. After being defeated by Sir Nicholas the wrestler sets one more challenge *'...to raise my donkey good, you'll treat him as a ball, and then throw him, saddled too, over the deer-park wall.'* As you can imagine, Sir Nicholas, being a gallant and heroic knight, duly obliged and tossed the animal over the wall. Being a generous soul too, *'...gives the Cornishman a heavy purse of gold.'*

The house was also famous for its Jacobean Falling Gardens, Old Deer Park, and its magnificent oak trees, the oldest of which was depicted in a stain glass window in the Chapel. When it blew down in a great storm in the 1600s it was made into a huge oak table – a shovel board. It was said to be the longest piece of furniture in the world, measuring 42 feet long; made from a single plank six inches thick. However, a piece was cut off the end when it was relocated to the Orangery in Tredegar House, where it can still be seen today. A devastating fire eventually forced the Kemeys-Tynte family

A view from the tower crane after all the debris had been cleared from the building.

to sell Cefn Mably to Lord Tredegar in 1924, who made it into an isolation hospital for tuberculosis patients.

Like so many large old buildings, subsequent owners have stamped their own mark on the place. I imagine the first building was a timber frame Hall house a fraction of the size it is today. The oldest surviving parts of the house date from the 16th century. They extend between the front entrance door and up to the chapel, and includes the long gallery. Although the building is made of rubble stonework, its appearance would have been completely different. The whole building was covered with a roughcast render and limewashed. However, one of the advantages of this 'naked' appearance is how much easier it is to read and understand the different phases of building. For example, to the right of the front door is a continuous vertical joint, indicating where, in 1713, the building was substantially extended. The new building was Georgian in style, characterised by two rows of curved headed sash windows, and a deep cove under the eaves. Whilst they were extending the building they decided to modernise other areas too. So, to the left of this new wing the old stone framed windows were partially filled in and the row of new sash windows were extended into the old building. This remodelling that took place nearly 300 years ago was hidden behind the render, but today is clearly visible in the exposed stonework. A major restoration was started in 1850 and this may have been when the courtyard was added behind the Georgian wing. The 1924 conversion also brought other small extensions and modifications to complete the building.

We were fortunate to find a series of high quality photographs published in a 1908 edition of Country Life magazine, and the Local Authority had also taken record photographs several years before the fire.

This is not the first ruinous old building I've worked on, and people often ask 'where do you begin with something like this'. It's quite simple really. You take a methodical approach, a lot of careful planning, and sympathetic design. It is important to adopt a strong philosophy from the outset, understanding why you are doing things, and justifying your approach. I always start with research – learn as much about the building as you can. This involves trawling through the archives for old photographs, drawings, and any other useful documents. We were fortunate to find a series of high quality photographs published in a 1908 edition of Country Life magazine, and the Local Authority had also taken record photographs several years before the fire. Although the building was badly damaged, there is a great deal of information that can be extracted from the ruins, such as mouldings on old timber windows, and a small remnant of the coved eaves, that enabled us to rebuild it exactly as it was. One thing I was determined to do was to get the contractors on board with the whole 'conservation' idea.

So I arranged to give them all, including the labourers, a brief talk about the history of the building and why it was important, and the careful approach we were taking. Most of the workmen appreciated being involved in something like this, and they would often approach me on site to talk about the building and what they had learned. They seemed proud to be part of it.

This was to be one of the most exclusive developments in Wales and Meadgate Homes were determined to get it right. The designs for the conversion were changed several times in order to maximise the potential of the house, but also to try and interpret the market demands of such a

Left: The restored courtyard with its variety of stone and timber windows.
Above: The Hall with paintings built in to its panelling. These are now restored into new panelling.

unique development. This was a huge risk for the developer – he was entering unchartered territory.

During the design period it was discovered that some paintings belonging to the house were being sold at an auction in Bristol. I was asked to verify that they belonged to Cefn Mably, so they could be held in storage until they were reinstated. Cadw insisted they were put back in the building where they belonged, in a public space, and not in one of the apartments. These were panel paintings – they were part of a panelled Hall at Cefn Mably, three of them located over doors, and one over a mantle piece. My plan was to rebuild the oak panelled Hall, providing the opportunity to present the paintings as they should be. I felt the room could be used as a communal space for residents to use for functions, meetings, birthday parties etc. but my client didn't agree and insisted that the Hall be divided up into another apartment. So, behind the front entrance door I created a small panelled reception room – and that's where the paintings have been installed.

The courtyard windows probably best represent the philosophy I adopted at Cefn Mably. Many of the walls surrounding the courtyard were in a very poor condition. Some had collapsed and some had to be pulled down.

All the windows had been lost. From remnants that did survive, and a series of photographs taken some time before the fire, I was able to deduce the variety of window styles that there had been. These were a mixture of 17th century cross-mullioned oak windows with leaded lights, more than one type of 19th century casement window, and a pair of small stone windows. With so much damage it would have been easy to start again, and unify all the windows. But I felt it was right to restore this courtyard to the period just before the fire, preserving the eclectic nature that reflects the many changes this building has undergone over the centuries.

Many of the windows at the rear of the building are 19th century timber casements, framed by stone mullions. In order to maintain a certain amount of symmetry they originally introduced a 'dummy' window next to one corner of the building. The stone frame and mullions were blocked and rendered with a blank panel. It always looked a bit conspicuous to me, so I thought it would be fun to introduce some *Trompe L'oeil* to give the impression that the window does exist. The success of this idea relies on the skill of the artist to convey realism to the painted fake window. I'm happy to say he made a really good job of the painting, and now you have to look twice to notice the window is not real.

One of the greatest design challenges was how to convert the two storey long gallery, with its soldier's gallery on the ground floor and a dancing gallery above.

One of the greatest design challenges was how to convert the two storey long gallery, with its soldier's gallery on the ground floor and a dancing gallery above. Of particular interest is the long narrow space on the first floor with its vaulted ceiling and many windows facing south. Originally the west end of this space was open to the air, with an oak framed screen offering the only security. This looked extremely tatty with rotting joints and blistering paint. But under the paint was a very old and robust timber screen, and I was convinced that with some careful restoration this could look magnificent. Unfortunately my client didn't agree and ordered that it should be consigned to the skip. One day, on seeing the oak screen in the skip, I hastily retrieved it, with some help, and sent it to a joinery workshop for cleaning and repair. The screen helped me solve the problem of how to

Gateway to the courtyard. The roof, guttering, timber windows, and parts of the stonework have all been replaced.

The entrance to the gallery over a new wooden bridge. The stone window was converted into an entrance door with lettering cut into the stonework above.

avoid dividing up the first floor space. The single long room now contains a dining space (next to the kitchen), a living area and, on the other side of the open screen, is the study. The whole space can still be read as one continuous Gallery, as it was always intended. We also discovered what appeared to be a small gaol (affectionately known as the 'dungeon') that we converted into a mini-gym. This apartment definitely has the 'wow' factor. The existing layout of the building made it difficult to access all areas. As Cefn Mably was built on sloping ground I was able to introduce two timber bridges that give access directly to a number of first floor apartments – one of them being the Gallery. These are the only two external additions I made to the entire building.

When converting churches or chapels I think it is essential that the feeling of open space is retained and not completely lost in the conversion.

The Chapel at the west end of the building is where it all started for me many years ago, so I was particularly keen to get this one right. When converting churches or chapels I think it is essential that the feeling of open space is retained and not completely lost in the conversion. This is not always easy, but with some careful thought and imagination it is often achievable. A new mezzanine floor was introduced at one end only, so that the entire roof structure is still open and completely visible as one. The kitchen was placed under the new floor, leaving the remainder of the Chapel as a living/dining space. The other bedroom was put into an attached building at the upper level. Alan and Jackie Crabbe were the first to move into Cefn Mably House, making the Chapel their new home. I am always nervous when people finally move into one of my buildings as I can only stand back and watch how they furnish the place. I was so relieved to see that they had excellent taste, using contemporary pieces to contrast with the traditional ecclesiastical building. I struck up a good relationship with Alan and Jackie, and they recently commissioned me to add more space to the Chapel apartment. This has just been completed and, as the Chapel is so 'architectural' I felt a subtle approach was called for. So the extension is a modest 'comfortable' little building that is more about function than form.

Below: The restored oak screen at one end of the gallery.
Right: Can you spot the dummy window?

One of the pleasing things to have emerged from of the whole project is how a new community has grown from the ashes of that fateful day in 1994. Most of the residents of the 13 apartments get together regularly for parties and meetings, making Cefn Mably more than just a collection of dwellings. Maybe it's the people, or is it the house? Whatever the reason I am happy to have been a small part of Cefn Mably's history.
I wonder if our paths will meet again!

Under the paint was a very old and robust timber screen, and I was convinced that with some careful restoration this could look magnificent.

Dummy windows

Artist, John Whally, paints the dummy window.

Also known as 'blind' windows, they became popular in 18th century when in 1696, William III of England introduced a type of property tax that required owners of houses with more than six windows to pay a levy. This unpopular tax persisted until 1851, and was said to be a tax on light and ventilation. Some believe it gave rise to the phrase 'daylight robbery'. However, some designers saw the opportunity to incorporate dummies into their designs as a means of maintaining symmetry in a façade, or continuing the rhythm of window openings. This could be achieved without actually providing a window, where internally it wasn't practical to do so. They simply built a rectangular recess into the façade to provide the impression of a window opening.

As the idea developed it became popular to paint a fake image of a window onto the blocked up opening, and some even added curtains, potted plants or an image of a cat sitting in the window. At Piercefield House near Chepstow, a real timber sash window, complete with glazing, was placed in front of the blocked opening for added realism.

16 Sarn Badrig
Where angels tip-toe across the sea

Perched high above the cliffs overlooking the sweeping sands of Cardigan Bay, with views out over the Irish Sea and the Llŷn Peninsula, Sarn Badrig is a modest little house with unusual connections. Whilst driving along the main coast road just south of Harlech you could easily pass by this little house without giving it a second glance. The house on its own doesn't stand out. It is a bungalow with white render and metal windows, but combined with the stunning view and the story behind the making of this house, Sarn Badrig is a unique and special place.

Set on the coast overlooking miles of sandy beach just south of Harlech.

The house gets its name from one of three reefs that stretch out into the bay towards Ireland – hence 'Sarn Badrig' or 'St Patrick's Causeway'. At low tide some of the reef protrudes above the water, and legend has it that angels tip-toe across from Ireland at night. Legend maybe, but it all adds to the magic of the place, its very name conjures up thoughts of a Tolkien fantasy.

I met up with Gwilym and Pat Hughes who have owned Sarn Badrig for 23 years and explained how they came across the house. They had been visiting Harlech regularly for about three years staying in other people's holiday homes. They decided they should buy a place for themselves and were told that the house was up for sale by a friend. It was just what their young family wanted – sea, sand and a simple life. They became the first Welsh owners of the house. Pat immersed herself in researching the

The pretty little house is so well positioned it must boast one of the best views in Wales.

The four and a half mile long beach stretches north to Portmerion, with the Llŷn Peninsula sweeping around to the west.

BULL·STREET·FRONTAGE

CORPORATION·St·FRONTAGE

BARROW'S·STORES·＊·1924

Pat wrote to Cadburys and sent them a picture of Sarn Badrig, asking if they knew the house.

Above: An engraving of Barrow Stores in Birmingham.
Right: Barn Sadrig nestles into its beautiful garden, with the winter stone seat perched on the south west corner.

house and had heard that the hotel, a hundred yards up the coast, had a connection with the house. The Birmingham-based chocolate makers Cadburys, bought Hafod Wen in 1922 as a convalescing home for their workers. Thus started a long relationship between Cadburys and Harlech, which remains today. Pat wrote to Cadburys and sent them a picture of Sarn Badrig, asking if they knew the house. About three weeks later she had a very nice letter from Sir Adrian Cadbury, saying he knew the house well, and had actually been there. It was built by his cousin, Harrison Barrow.

A secluded entrance provides a sheltered spot on those blustery days. Note the thick Cornish slates on the roof.

Harrison Barrow was a prominent businessman and local politician based in the Midlands. He had inherited the family department store, which at one time was the place to shop in Birmingham. It sold high quality goods and provided a high quality service. It started as a tea and coffee shop owned by two Cadbury brothers, who decided to go into the manufacture of chocolate, and the shop passed down to a nephew Richard Cadbury Barrow. Cadburys were renowned for being one of the most philanthropic companies towards their workers. Lord Cadbury was a devoted Quaker and built his company into a successful business and still managed to maintain his altruistic ideals. The factories were light and airy, cigarettes and alcohol were banned, and workers were provided with all manner of athletic activities. The Bournville Village created by Cadburys for their workers provided sporting clubs and social, educational, and medical facilities. It was an idyllic model village where everyone was happy; and when you became unwell you could convalesce in Hafod Wen.
When Cadburys had their two week shut-down in summer, virtually the whole of Bournville came to Harlech, it was like a big family holiday. There was even a train that ran directly from the Village to Harlech.

When Cadburys had their two week shut-down in summer, virtually the whole of Bournville came to Harlech, it was like a big family holiday.

Sarn Badrig is built into the sloping land so that, when you approach it from the road, you are looking at the roof popping up above the variety of shrubs that surround the building. A flight of steps takes you down to the front door in the corner of the L shaped building that is a perfect little haven and sun trap. The construction is fairly conventional for between-the-wars architecture, when materials were still in short supply and modern forms of design and new materials were starting to take off.
All the materials and labour were brought in from the Midlands, no doubt using workmen they were familiar with. The walls are white rendered with steel 'Crittal' windows and the roof is covered with half inch thick Cornish slate. Strange considering the worlds best slates are made in north Wales. Perhaps they just wanted to be a little different, or maybe they didn't want to be 'Welsh'. Some of the greatest buildings in Britain have adopted materials from far off places, just to show off, just because they can.

Above: The living
room with its minimal
detailing, and large
slate fireplace.
Right: Simple oak door
latch, and the stone
steps that lead down
to the front door.

Nevertheless, the combination of materials works beautifully.
The plan layout of the building is very simple and yet perfect for its
location. All rooms are designed for the view, only the corridor and
bathroom are facing away from it. The bedrooms and living room have
breathtaking views over the sea, whilst the kitchen door opens out to views
of the four and a half mile stretch of sandy beach extending north towards
Portmerion. Its styling is reminiscent of the Arts & Crafts movement with
the use of high quality natural materials without the need for fussy design.
Simple details – beautifully crafted. All floors throughout the house are
covered with oak. The doors are also oak, and have beautifully tactile
oak latches – something more common in an historic medieval dwelling.
Although I can't make my mind up about the living room ceiling, which is
leaning towards 'Art Deco' with its slightly stepped recess and concealed
strip lighting. It doesn't quite fit and makes you feel like you're in the
foyer of a 1930s cinema. But then with this setting you could be in a movie
– maybe it is fitting after all. The only real changes the Hughes family have
made to the house are the new kitchen units. These are painted timber
units and sit quite comfortably with the style of the house.

A young woman on her honeymoon at Sarn Badrig sitting in the original window, which slides wide open.

The metal windows have caused some debate in the Hughes household. Should they stay or should they go? They are extremely draughty, particularly when the wind rolls in off the Irish Sea. But they are so much part of the house and its character. I was able to present a good 'conservation' argument to Pat who I think was swayed, and I am confident they will be retained. Adding very small draught excluders is possible and will improve the problem greatly. It would be such a shame to sacrifice them. Whilst walking along the west side of the house overlooking the Irish Sea, Pat showed me the big picture window of the living room, and explained that it also used to be a metal window in four sections and opened out fully by sliding and folding to each end. She described a picture she has of a woman on her honeymoon, sitting on the sill of the window enjoying the view. She looked very happy. Just below the window is a bench Pat embarrassingly referred to as the 'gin and tonic' seat. I wonder why! It is located in such a position that you get a perfect view in summer of the sun setting over the Irish sea. There is another seat further south at the corner of the building, and set into the bank. This faces the sunset in winter, but is surrounded by stone walls that shelter you from the bracing winter winds.

Harrison Barrow kept Sarn Badrig until his death in 1953, and Pat believes it is important to keep his traditions alive, and she keeps a photograph of him hanging on the living room wall. The house was built as a holiday home and remains that way today, as it always has. She also maintains the connection with Cadburys by placing a small bar of Cadburys chocolate on everyone's pillow; and when children come there's always a bowl full of chocolates – and they say 'can we go back to the chocolate house'.

Sarn Badrig is definitely a case of 'less is more' with the house having such a simple design. But the view gives you so much 'more' and is the real making of this house. Pat has a friend who travels a lot with her work, and has visited some of the most beautiful places in the world. She has no hesitation in saying this is one of the best views she has ever seen. Pat says "every time you come here it's a new time. You come through the gate and it's freedom, it's magic. It's such a beautiful place".

Cantre'r Gwaelod – The Lost Land of Wales

Cantre'r Gwaelod was said to cover much of the lowlands now beneath Cardigan Bay. Single ridges of several miles run at roughly right angles to the shore in the north of the Bay. One of these is Sarn Badrig. Legend states that these ridges are the remains of causeways built to give access to the present mainland at high tide, but in reality, they are the remains of glacial moraines – formations of gravel, clay and boulders left behind at the end of the last Ice Age.

There are many versions of the story that explains how this area came to be reclaimed by the sea. In the legends known and told today, the land is called Cantre'r Gwaelod. It was ruled by Gwyddno Garanhir (Longshanks), born circa 520AD. The land was said to be extremely fertile. The kingdom depended on a dyke to protect it from the sea. Sluice gates were opened at low tide to drain water from the land, and closed as the tide returned. A character called Seithennin features in many stories of how the land drowned. In some, he is a friend of the king and the appointed watchman of the sluice gates. One night a storm blew up. Seithennin had fallen asleep due to too much wine. The sluice gates were left open and the sea rushed in, drowning the land. The king and some of his followers escaped by running along Sarn Cynfelin. Another version states that Seithennin was a local visiting king. As the storm blew up, he was amorously distracting the maiden who was in charge of the sluice gates. The maiden was unable to shut the gates and the land flooded. It is said that the church bells of Cantre'r Gwaelod ring out in times of danger.

The perfect location on
the west Wales coast.

17 Forge Row, Cwmavon
Building a future for our past

This little row of ironworkers cottages form a very important part of historic buildings conservation in Wales, and is now the best surviving terrace of industrial housing in the South Wales Valleys, possibly in the UK. I was particularly pleased to film this row of buildings as it was an opportunity to tell the story of how a Building Preservation Trust operates.

A couple of miles south of Blaenavon at the entrance to a World Heritage Site.

These are the unsung heroes of historic buildings preservation, working tirelessly with no rewards, and very little praise. In my work as a conservation architect I often come across this tenacious group of people, with some projects taking many years to get off the ground. But Forge Row is probably one of the most significant projects in Wales.

Forge Row was built in 1804 for the men working at the now demolished Varteg Forge across the road. The Forge served the nearby Blaenavon Ironworks, which became one of the largest exporters of iron in the world. It was founded in 1788 by three businessmen from the Midlands – Thomas Hill, Benjamin Pratt and Thomas Hopkins. They utilised the very latest industrial technology with three blast furnaces operated by steam power. Such was the significance of Blaenavon's industrial landscape, it was designated a World Heritage Site in November 2000.

Building housing near the workplace benefited both the employer and his workforce. With such a short walk to the Forge it meant that the men arrived for work fresh and fit each day and there was no excuse for being late. This was a key geographic change in Wales, brought on by the industrial revolution. Prior to this the vast majority of the workforce in Wales were engaged in agriculture and cottage industries, and were dispersed all over the Welsh countryside. As people started leaving the

What could be more Welsh – a terrace of cottages built amongst the hills in the South Wales Valleys.

Although the cottages have small back yards, the front gardens are extremely long.

countryside to go where the work was, the greatest challenge facing the iron and coal industries was how to house their workforce.

Large conurbations were growing rapidly around places of industry. Initially the housing provided was very poor and people lived with squalor and disease until the introduction of the Public Health Act in 1848; and it took many years before people saw the benefits of the new Act.

The houses at Forge Row were actually of a very high standard. Most workers were living in no more than hovels at the time. Skilled workmen were hard to come by and it made sense to provide a good standard of accommodation for men and women who were one of your main assets and therefore an essential part of your business. It was therefore a great benefit to the employers that their workers remained healthy and didn't have far to travel to work. This ensured that output in the factories remained efficient. Forge Row were probably the first terraced houses to have back doors, and remained unique in this respect until about 1825 (British Ironworks Houses at Abersychan were next to have back doors). Most companies built their workers houses to a set pattern. At Forge Row there were originally 12 cottages, with the two end units providing a bakery and a laundry. Imagine having your own bakery and

Below: No.1 Forge Row. The house between the two chimneys once contained two cottages. With a bakery and laundry attached to each end of the terrace.

laundry in the same terrace, it must have seemed a luxury. The buildings were constructed of finely coursed rubble stone walls decorated with limewash, wooden double casement windows (although these may have been iron originally) and ledged and battened doors, all under a slate roof laid in diminishing courses. It is really nice to see the elegant little gutter brackets still surviving just under the eaves and, of course, made of iron. Inside they were 2 up 2 down, with the walls lime plastered and colour washed. The stairs were narrow and steep, and were more like a ladder than stairs. Even though these were the model of luxury for the workers at that time, the cottages were still very cramped and overcrowded.

Varteg Forge only operated for ten years (and then again between 1823-40) closing as a result of poor transport links to the coast and the introduction of steel.

The importance of Forge Row was finally confirmed when the cottages were listed in 1973. But by the early 1980s they had fallen into a perilous condition. The Local Authority were poised to demolish the terrace, despite their statutory protection, but were saved at the 11th hour by The British

The Local Authority were poised to demolish the terrace, despite their statutory protection, but were saved at the 11th hour by The British Historic Buildings Preservation Trust.

Historic Buildings Preservation Trust. The Trust operates as a charity whose sole aim is to rescue historic buildings from ruin, and put them to a beneficial new use. Thomas Lloyd, Chairman of the Trust, was the driving force behind this heroic act and has become one of Wales' most vociferous champions of the plight of historic buildings under threat in Wales. He first highlighted the problem over 20 years ago when he published his book entitled 'The Lost Houses of Wales'.

The Trust prepared a feasibility study to show that, with the help of financial grants and cheap loans, which are not available to the private or commercial world, the Trust were able to restore the buildings and sell them without making a loss. Unlike a developer they do not need to make a profit, so the figures tend to stack up a little easier. The Trust also made a pledge – they would only be sold to local people and not become holiday cottages. As Tom explains "We don't have to repay the grants when the job is done. We sell the buildings net of the grant and that tips the balance in favour of getting it done usually with just a tiny surplus".

The basic remit of the Trust is to take on buildings where they are no longer viable. As the buildings are often listed, the extra cost of building work, using conservation materials and methods, often exceeds the value of the building when completed, effectively giving the building a negative value.

During the rescue, a scheme was devised that would make significant alterations to the terrace, but not in a way that would harm their historic character, and that is the key to good conservation. It's about the management of change. If the restoration of these little cottages was to be sustainable they had to be brought up to a standard that is acceptable today. I am a strong believer that we should live with the past not in the past. Conservation is about breathing new life into old buildings whilst retaining their intrinsic historic value. At Forge Row this was achieved by simply knocking two cottages into one, effectively doubling the space of each dwelling. The only real sign of this change is in the arrangement of the front doors. All the original front doors have been retained but every other door is painted a different colour so that the present front door is

The hall inside the front door. As the cottage was doubled in size, there are stairs at each end.

Above: The spacious living room was once divided into two or three rooms.
Below: 'Trixie'.

clearly identifiable. Behind the other doors, quite cleverly, are the metre cupboards. The subtlety of the restoration is a triumph. Lime washed stone walls, Welsh slate roofs, and wooden windows – simple and effective. It's now a beautiful row of cottages in a peaceful setting.

I visited Eric and Carole at No.1 Forge Row. They have lived there for 18 years. They were living in Bassaleg and Eric was teaching at Rougemant School in Newport, when he heard a colleague raving about these cottages in Cwmavon. They made a visit and instantly fell in love with them. They were asked to put in a sealed bid for one of the newly restored cottages but had no idea what it was worth, so they just took a guess and were successful with their offer of £62,251. It was a lot of money in 1988 as Carol recalls. "We put our shirt on it because we wanted it so bad. It was like winning a house in a raffle. The house stays cool in Summer and is very cosy in Winter, particularly with the open fire. I love the little low windows upstairs when you wake up in the morning because you're in the countryside. On a good Summer night you'll see three or four of us sitting out on the wall with a drink. It's such a lovely place to live."

The Trust were careful to preserve the exteriors as they found them, and as people come up from Pontypool into the World Heritage Site this is the

The typically small cottage window to the bedroom, frames the view over the countryside.

first significant thing they see. What could set off the whole mêlée of this World Heritage Site more appropriately?

Limewash

Most of us expect to see old buildings with their bare stone walls, exposing the warmth of the natural local stone. Yet, it is only in relatively recent years that exposed stonework has become fashionable. Prior to the Victorian period, most ordinary rubble stone walls would have been covered up with either lime plaster, or limewash. Limewash was commonly called 'whitewash' on account of it being white in its natural state, before any pigments were added. Lime comes from burning limestone rock at over 1,000 degrees centigrade, converting it into chalk. It is then 'slaked' by adding water to it, and when cooled and left for several weeks it turns into a white buttery material, called lime putty. Sand is now added to make mortar and plaster, or simply watered down to make limewash.

18 Ceunant
The potter's fairytale cottage

Now for something completely different! This little cottage is as much a place of work as it is a home. A building that has materialised out of its surroundings and reflects the natural environment within which it is built. It has survived destruction on more than one occasion, yet it is so serene that it feels as if it has grown out of the ground.

Set in a Snowdonia forest, near Llanwst.

'Ceunant' was built by Vicky Buxton and Philip Owen, a potter and engineer with a passion and determination that is only matched by the sheer presence of the place, a place that would befit any Hans Christian Anderson story. Tucked away in a Snowdonia forest, the cottage is lucky to be here at all. When Vicky and Philip first saw the cottage, it was no more than a pile of stones.

When they lost their home in the 1980s to a new road scheme they saw the cottage for sale in an estate agent's window for just £13,000. They cheekily made an offer of £9,000, which was immediately accepted. Unfortunately they didn't realise the previous owner had a long running battle with the planning authorities and the building was immune from action.

Its designated use as a dwelling had expired, and it would require planning consent if it was to be lived in again. Philip decided to carry on regardless, an action he says, in hindsight, he would not do again. After many long years of discussion and argument with the authorities, he managed to get his retrospective planning consent. The £25,000 they had sold their house for was all they had to live off for three years whilst they built the house and workshop. It paid, not only for their living expenses, but also all the materials for the building project. A remarkable achievement!

These unusual windows not only help put the building in context but also provide an evocative silhouette when seen from inside the building.

Above: The house is built into the hillside and sits comfortably within the woodland setting.

Being saved from dereliction by Vicky and Philip wasn't the first time Ceunant was saved unexpectedly. The little cottage was saved from destruction once before. Back in 1925 a dam disaster saw millions of tons of water crash through Dolgarrog. One Saturday night two reservoirs high up the valley burst open. Many buildings were completely destroyed but Ceunant was one of the few that remained standing. Amazingly the loss of life was relatively low. Many villagers were at a film show and 200 people were working late in the nearby aluminium factory. Incredibly the final death toll was just 16, even though the village was almost completely wiped out. Sixty years on Ceunant cottage had fallen into disrepair, and it really was looking like the end of the road. In fact, if it wasn't for Philip's oversight in realising the seriousness of the planning difficulties, and carrying on regardless, this cottage simply would not exist. It would have, by now, been totally engulfed by nature.

Right: Inside the entrance porch.
The doors and windows bend and twist like trees to reflect the woodland outside.
Below left: Close up shot of Dragon clay ridge tile made by Vicky.

At the centre of this adventurous project is a pottery workshop, with a small display room for the finished pots at the extreme end of the building. But which came first, the home or the pottery? The cottage at the other end is their home, so naturally came first. But the concept of a work place for the potter seems to have been the driving force behind the project, with living space playing second fiddle. Above the workshop, in the roof is a large 'T' shaped living room, but it is not accessible from the main cottage, and the rest of the living accommodation. You have to go outside, up a small stairs at the back of the property, and through a hatch in the floor. This kind of arrangement suggests the potter's workshop has always been the priority, and the living room in the roof, almost an afterthought. Whilst the layout of the building doesn't quite work, this is more than made up for by the detail and features lovingly crafted into the building. Living in such a beautiful area, deep in the forest is an added joy.

Left: The original tiny cottage can be seen behind with its blue windows and fascias. All the new timberwork is left in its natural state.
Above left: Carefully selected natural stones help blend the building into the landscape.
Above right: A feature gable window with balconette sits over the large pottery workshop doors. Philip and Vicky are very proud of their stonework.

Vicky explained that they came from a busy town on a main road. The view from her workshop was a blank brick wall, and she was dying to get out into the countryside, so coming to Ceunant was a real treat. They were very enthusiastic and it was the dream they had always wanted – to live in harmony with nature. They were very idealistic, needed somewhere to live and work, so the idea of a country pottery and selling what they made from their door in a beautiful setting was always part of their plans.

They have constructed the whole building themselves, learning new skills along the way. They started at the back, out of the way, where they could make their mistakes. As they progressed to the front of the house their masonry skills were fully developed, and you have to say it has been executed to an extremely high standard. As they got into the roof and other woodwork Philip's artistic side started to evolve. It became more elaborate as his confidence grew. The main feature of the house is the amazing tree mullioned windows. It is not hard to see where the inspiration came from as the site is buried in a forest of trees. It is quite extraordinary standing inside the house looking out through one of these windows at the real trees beyond and the dappled sunlight created by the canopy of leaves. Philip modestly explains how he just cut them out with a jigsaw.

Left: The double height display space helps show off Vicky's work, where it is sold as part of a small cottage industry.

Above: The living room above the pottery workshop. The shape and natural light in the room makes this a very cosy space.

I'm sure there's more to it than that Philip!

There are artistic elements all over the building. The ends of the roof fascias have dragons heads carved into them; the clay ridge tiles are not unexpectedly made by Vicky, the ends are again dragons heads, where small birds creep inside to make their nest. The theme continues as little dragons wrap themselves around the clay chimney pots. Wherever you look there is a little feature or detail that catches your eye, conveying that unique sense of a well crafted building; a piece of artwork made for living and working in. I noticed inside the old cottage, a bedroom window sill with wavy layers of different coloured woods. Philip explained that it reflects the profile of the mountains that can be seen through this particular window.

Vicky and Philip speak passionately about their home and what they've created, remembering where each piece of stone was salvaged from. They care very much about the environment, so building cheaply also

Below: Vicky, doing what she loves best – making pottery in her very own workshop, with the countryside just outside the door.

satisfied their need to limit the demands upon the planets scarce resources. What better way to build than with local and salvaged materials.

Building a home is a very personal affair, and it's not always possible to realise your dream when it has been designed and built by others. And yet how many people can have the imagination and vision to create a building that suits them perfectly? What Ceunant represents is a building made by two very creative people, that shows off their individual skills and personalities – the very essence of Vicky and Philip are in this building. How many of us can say that about our own home?

Vicky and Philip's story is one of mistakes, tenacity, and artistic endeavour. Their passion has driven them on for many years through hard times – it has been one enormous labour of love from start to finish. From all this they have created a unique little building that seems to

Building a home is a very personal affair, and it's not always possible to realise your dream when it has been designed and built by others.

Above: Two crafts combine. Philip's imaginative woodwork, and Vicky's artistic pottery.

grow out of the hillside, deep in the woods. The idea of building your own home from where you live and work has a very simple and natural appeal, something man has been doing for many centuries. But today, with regulation and legislation it is one of the most difficult things to do, as Vicky and Philip found out.

The building is now complete and Philip is planning his next project. Vicky finds it very rewarding selling pieces of pottery from her showroom at home – a dream come true! (www.claywales.co.uk)

Index

Credits

Photographers

Published by Graffeg
First published 2007
Copyright © Graffeg 2007
ISBN 978-1-905582-13-6

Graffeg, Radnor Court,
256 Cowbridge Road East,
Cardiff CF5 1GZ Wales UK.
Tel: +44 (0)29 2037 7312
sales@graffeg.com
www.graffeg.com

Graffeg are hereby identified as the authors of this work in accordance with section 77 of the Copyrights, Designs and Patents Act 1988.

Distributed by the
Welsh Books Council
www.cllc.org.uk
castellbrychan@cllc.org.uk

A CIP Catalogue record for this book is available from the British Library.

Designed and produced by
Peter Gill & Associates
sales@petergill.com
www.petergill.com

All rights reserved. No part of this publication may be reproduced, stored in a retrieval system or transmitted, in any form or by any means, electronic, mechanical, photocopying, recording or otherwise, without the prior permission of the publishers Graffeg.

Discovering Welsh Houses written by Michael Davies.

The publishers are also grateful to the Welsh Books Council for their financial support and marketing advice. www.gwales.com

Every effort has been made to ensure that the information in this book is current and it is given in good faith at the time of publication.

By arrangement with Alfresco Television.

By arrangement with the BBC
BBC logo © BBC 1996.
The BBC logo is a registered trademark of the British Broadcasting Corporation and is used under licence.

The author wishes to thank Liz Lloyd-Griffiths of Alfresco Television and Martyn Ingram of the BBC for their continued support.

All photographs by Michael Davies except the following:
Andrew Davies 18-25; Glamorgan Record Office 28; Courtesy of Mary Clark 29; Gareth Davies Photography 48 - 51; Zander Olsen 72/73; Jean Napier 74, 75; Loyn & Co. 96, 98, 102, 103, 105; Neil Turner 146, 152, 155, 157, 158; Country Life Picture Library 149, 153; Courtesy of Pat Hughes 164, 169 (black and white photo).

Further reading

Wales

The Buildings of Wales Series:

- *T Lloyd, J Orbach & R Scourfield* for *Cadw* Carmarthenshire and Ceredigion
- *T Lloyd, J Orbach & R Scourfield* for *Cadw* Pembrokeshire
- *Edward Hubbard* for Cadw Clwyd (Denbighshire & Flintshire)
- *John Newman* for Cadw Gwent/ Monmouthshire
- *John Newman* for Cadw Glamorgan
- *Richard Haslam* Powys

- *Peter Smith* Houses of the Welsh Countryside
- *John B Hilling* The Historic Architecture of Wales
- *CADW* Traditional Agricultural Buildings in Wales – Care and Conservation
- *CADW* Converting Historic Farm Buildings in Wales – A Guide to Good Practice
- *CADW* Industrial Workers' Housing in Wales – Care and Conservation
- *CADW* Small Rural Dwellings in Wales – Care and Conservation
- *Jeremy Lowe* Welsh Industrial Workers Housing 1775–1875
- *Jeremy Lowe* Welsh Country Workers Housing 1775~1875
- *Martin Davies* Save the last of the magic.... Traditional Qualities of the West Wales Cottage
- *Iorwerth C. Peate* The Welsh House
- *Christopher Day* Places of the Soul

- *Pat Borer & Cindy Harris* The Whole House Book – Ecological Building Design & Materials
- *Thomas Lloyd* The Lost Houses of Wales – A Survey of Country Houses in Wales Demolished Since c.1900
- *Richard Suggett* Houses & History in the March of Wales – Radnorshire 1400~1800

General

- *Alec Clifton-Taylor* The Pattern of English Building
- *Mark Girouard* Life in the English Country House – A Social and Architectural History.
- *Mark Girouard* The Victorian Country House
- *Anthony Quiney* Period Houses
- *Anthony Quiney* House and Home
- *Stephen Calloway* The Elements of Style
- *John Summerson* Architecture in Britain 1530 –1830